Islam, Liberty, and Development

Islam, Liberty, and Development

by Mohammad Khatami

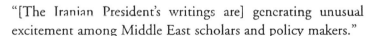

"[The Iranian President's writings are] generating unusual excitement among Middle East scholars and policy makers."
— *The New York Times*

Institute of Global Cultural Studies
Binghamton University
1998

Published by the Institute of Global Cultural Studies
Binghamton University, Binghamton, NY 13902-6000.

Library of Congress Cataloging-in-Publication Data
Khatami, Mohammad, 1942-
        Islam, Liberty, and Development / by Mohammad
Khatami
        p.   cm.
        1. Iranian Politics. 2. Islam and Modernity. 3. Iran. 4.
Islamic Revolution. 5. Islam and the West

ISBN 1-883058-83-X

Distributed by Global Publications, IGCS
Binghamton University, State University of New York
Binghamton, NY, USA 13902-6000
☎ (607) 777-4495. Fax: (607) 777-6132
e-mail: pmorewed@binghamton.edu
http://ssips.binghamton.edu

Table of Contents ∾

Introduction ᴄᴧᴏ

This book is a reflection of the intellectual concerns of its author with the demands of religious belief in the modern era, a subject that reverberates today on three different levels in the discourse of the Muslim world, affecting elites and the masses alike.

On the individual level, the question pertains to how a person can accept the demands and consequences of modern thought and practice while simultaneously maintaining a religious identity. The test of possessing this religious identity is either being acknowledged as belonging to the community of believers, or at least, a private admission of being religious that the individual is content with.

When it comes to society as a whole, the puzzle that has stirred intellectual and practical ferment among Muslims is how we can create a religious society that is also responsive to the demands of today's world, capable of providing welfare, social justice, development, and freedom to its people.

On the level of civilizations, the main question has been whether history has come to an end, whether from now on the destiny of humans must be confined to the destiny of Western civilization, or whether there is a future way for humanity outside Western civilization, a way that has a separate origin from the West and a separate destination.

This three-level encounter of religious thought with modernity is particularly important to Muslims. The dominant currents of thought in the Muslim world continue to see in Islam a religion that has a place in all facets of individual and, especially, social life. Religion is viewed as being present from before birth until after death. In the dominant view of Muslim "Sharia" — the practical laws that govern religious behavior — Islam is viewed as possessing unrivaled intellectual and practical insight, making it the only system that can effectively address the corresponding rights and duties of the individual and society. At the same time, it is amply clear that Muslim societies have not indigenously passed through a period of Reformation or secularization, and this represents one of the consequences of the ubiquity of the Sharia in the lives and thinking of Muslims.

Continuing the tradition of his other writings, Khatami discusses the requirements of religious belief in today's world on all three levels. His main focus, however, is on the interchange among civilizations. While he aims to clarify the issue of religiosity and modernism on the individual level and to shed light on the prerequisites of creating a progressive religious society, Khatami rejects the simplistic assumption that there are no alternatives to Western civilization in the process of development.

Khatami sees this as a complex and historically conditioned subject, one whose scrutiny requires a coordinated social effort. It is thus for good reason that he stays clear of the temptation to answer directly the key questions that he raises. In the tradition of Muslim philosophers, he believes that asking the right questions and asking questions in the right way, or clarifying the terms of the debate, are crucial for arriving at appropriate solutions to extant puzzles. On the basis of the historical experience of Muslims in various aspects of their practical and intellectual life, he preemptively exposes the shortcomings of secularism on the one hand, and retrograde religiosity on the other. He shows the absolute inability of the latter in defending the sanctity of religion.

As a religious thinker from a country that occupies a prominent place in Islamic thought, Khatami brings to light the concerns and questions that arise in the debate on religious intellectualism all over the Muslim world.

It was Mohammad Khatami and his thinking, after

all, that succeeded in attracting a people whose revolution was less than two decades old — a revolution that shook the world — and to amaze and surprise the pundits of Iranian society and politics. Thus, gaining familiarity with the views and positions of the current President of the Islamic Republic of Iran who aims to reconcile religion with democracy and development, and also to bring about harmony between religious belief and living in the current era, is compelling and important.

The English translations of the chapters entitled "Our Revolution and the Future of Islam," "Fears and Hopes," "Observations on the Information World," and "Covenant with the Nation," were previously published in the book *Hope and Challenge: The Iranian President Speaks* (IGCS, 1997). The other chapters of this book are translated texts of addresses delivered by Mr. Khatami in 1996 and 1997. Minor stylistic and editorial modifications have been made occasionally. It is hoped that this book makes an original contribution to cross-cultural understanding and dialogue.

Mohammad-Ali Abtahi
Director
Office of the President of the Islamic Republic of Iran

Islam, Liberty, and Development

Freedom and Development ∾

The Dar-Alfonun, Iran's first technical school of higher education, was inaugurated by Nasser-eddin Shah on the fifth of Rabi'I, 1268 AH (October 27, 1851). This event marked the birth of the idea of "development," as we know it in Iran today. Our intense preoccupation with defining development, and how we might achieve it a full century and a half after the founding of the school, shows that we have not achieved development. We must try to find out why.

Here I do not wish to address the complex idea of cultural development. I hope that the vision and effort of our eminent thinkers will take the ambiguity out of the meaning of development. Instead I wish to put forth a general discussion of the cultural prerequisites of development, not the meaning of development itself. In my view, development is a form of desirable transformation in society. In its contemporary meaning, development is merely one form of transformation. Three points are essential to consider.

First, no transformation will be humane and productive unless people knowingly and willingly participate in the process of that transformation. Second, the active and willing presence of humans in the process of development requires that serious and established thinking be present in large parts of society. Third, sustainable and productive thinking in society has to be based, first and foremost, on freedom.

Thus we cannot expect any positive transformations anywhere unless the yearning for freedom is fulfilled. That is the freedom to think and the security to express new thinking. The way I see it, development is a Western construct, and all those who seek development must become modern. This means that development as currently defined is a branch of the tree of modern civilization. If that civilization arrives, so will development. Indeed, those who claim that adopting Western thinking and values is a necessary precondition of development are not misguided. And alongside Western thinking and wisdom, the Western temperament and ethic must also be adopted.

But I also believe that development, as conceived today, is only one form of transformation and evolution in human society, not the only and exclusive version of it. Certainly this transformation and evolution has brought many benefits to humanity, but I believe that it has caused much harm as well. In looking at Western civilization and its idea of development, many realities have been overlooked and ignored with devastating consequences. We who discuss development today cannot go back four hundred years to the time when the West started the journey in order to get to where it is today. Instead, the vast experience of Westerners is before us, and if we are thoughtful, we must choose our future path on the basis of this experience. This means that we must see the strengths and shortcomings of the Western experience and to arrive at a better and more desirable choice.

Negating the exclusivity of progress in its current form, which has been called development, is not to deny the realities of modern civilization, and one can say with certainty that in any society that wants to advance, nothing instrumental will happen unless its people incorporate Western civilization's achievements, instead of trying to circumvent them. This requires that we become familiar with Western civilization, to be in touch with its spirit, which is modernity. Those who are not familiar with this spirit will never be able to effect positive change in their lives. Thus the main criterion of transformation is incorporating Western civilization into one's own thinking, and the goal of this familiarity with the West is understanding the main tenets of modernity, which is hidden behind many appearances. Sadly, nations such as we are still devoid of such understanding. As Abdulhadi Haeri has put it, we have yet to become familiar with the two countenances of Western civilization. Our encounter with the West has been mostly superficial. We have vacillated between the equally harmful extremes of either being taken in and entranced by the West, or loathing and rejecting it.

In my view the discussion of development requires a fundamental look at what Western civilization is and how we are related to it. If this debate begins in earnest, the debate on development will advance more rapidly and with greater certainty.

Why is it that a century and half after the creation of Dar-Alfonun, the mother of modern scientific schooling in Iran, we are still mired in the same question of what development is and why we haven't achieved it?

The attempt to answer this important question must begin by relating another historical anecdote: On Friday, the seventeenth of Rabi'I, 1268 AH (November 9, 1851), a mere twelve days after Dar-Alfonun was inaugurated, Nasser-Eddin Shah had Amirkabir — the very man by whose vision and wisdom that school was conceived — put to death in the Feen bathhouse in the city of Kashan. In my view the secret of our malaise lies therein.

Centuries of our history have been governed not by the effort and thoughtfulness of the people of this land, but by autocratic and whimsical rulers, and because of the existence of authoritarianism and its central role in our society, our people have not had the opportunity to be active in their own society. Freedom of thought, which is the highest emblem of being and the key condition of our presence on the stage of destiny, as well as the main impetus for growth and dynamism in life, has not been respected. In other words, the secret of our greatest historical problems, to borrow from Farabi, has been the dominance of deceit and craftiness on our destiny, a deceit that was already deeply rooted before the advent of Islam. Rampant corruption in pre-Islamic, Sasanid Iran had brought the country to the brink of explosion. With the coming of Islam, the foundations of deceit began to shake, but a mere 40 years after the coming of Islam, in the period known as the Rashed Caliphate, authoritarianism of a more dangerous form came to govern the destiny of the Islamic community, for this time authoritarianism and tyranny adopted the guise of Islamic legitimacy.

As Islamic civilization came to replace Sasanid Persian civilization or other civilizations, it was expected that the political manifestations of those civilizations would also be replaced. Especially at the beginning of Islamic civilization, there was much hope in the new political environment. The legitimacy of concepts such as collective decision making, reconciliation, and the supremacy of the public interest was upheld by the behavior of the prophet himself and to some extent by the Caliphs who succeeded him, especially by Imam Ali. A new horizon dawned over people. Had it been allowed to continue, it could have spurred serious thinking, and the Islamic community would have undoubtedly had a different destiny. But sadly, the dark shadow of tyranny began to dominate Muslims. Even more sadly, effort was put into passing this tyranny off as the pillar of the new way of life. The autocratic form of policy grew into a legacy, a relic that led to the decline and degradation of the civilization.

In such an atmosphere reflection about subjects' political destiny was stifled, and the only thinker who managed to dedicate deep thought to philosophy, politics, and civic discourse was Farabi, the founder of Islamic philosophy, with whom the idea begins and terminates at the same time. After him, thought left the sphere of secular affairs, and because of the dominance of despotism and its consequences, deep investigation became focused strictly on esoteric and metaphysical phenomena, and we see that despite the advancement of knowledge about the supernatural, philosophical thinking on politics, society, and different social spheres became almost entirely dormant.

Alongside metaphysical philosophy, another form of thinking, namely Sufism and mysticism, gained currency, especially among the elite. And although Sufism can be viewed in some instances as a response and complaint to unpleasant and hapless circumstances, it was a wrong and ill-fated response. Instead of challenging the bitterness of extant political reality and looking for a way of changing that reality through offering alternative realities and visions, Sufism, at least its extreme versions, resisted the dominant political order by negating the relevance of politics and political thought altogether. As Farabi has said, many from this camp put forth the proposition that real understanding and salvation could only come from negating all that pertains to this world, including civil society. This means that by rejecting and staying away from politics, they left society in the bloodstained hands of autocrats. Instead of resisting injustice, they closed their eyes, even though they did not cooperate with oppressors.

At the same time, a sort of insularity and parochialism began to dominate Muslims, and this marginalized even Islamic philosophy, as esoteric and metaphysical as it was. What gained prominence as political thought was a theoretical-practical system, apparently the creation of the famed Shafi'ite theologian of the Abbasid period and the chief magistrate of Baghdad, Abolhassan al-Mawardy, who wrote the important book *Al-Ahkam al-Soltaniyyah — Commandments of Kingship*. The Hanbalid interpretation of al-Mawardy was later put forward in a book with the same title by Abu 'Ali al-Farra'. These two books implicitly legitimized the extent of Abbasid authoritarianism and also proposed a system of laws based on Islamic thought for the governance of Muslim society, a society whose main pillar of organization was

Islamic jurisprudence. Yet religious law itself is dependent on thought, and does not in and of itself give form and function to thoughts. Where there is rational thinking in society, religious law will be vibrant, instrumental, and adaptive. Through rational thinking a jurisconsult can develop a system of law which is adaptive, appropriate, and effective. Instead, the religious law that was supposed to be based on rational thought became the basis of its form and function.

Concurrently, a different form of political thought gained currency which was in essence the revival of a previously examined pre-Islamic paradigm. Important thinkers such as Abolhassan 'Ameri and Moskuya helped bring back the pre-Islamic tradition of authoritarianism from ancient Persia. The work of Nezam al-Mulk and al-Ghazali (if the latter part of *Nasihat al-Moluk* could authentically be attributed to him) further solidified this thinking, turning into one of the main obstacles of serious thought for Muslims.

This was a very unfortunate development, but even sadder was the fact that Muslims took their hapless fate as manifest destiny, as the ineluctable work of God and nature, and after this people could not think beyond authoritarianism in the sphere of politics. People either submitted to this fate, or even if they thought of combating the extant authoritarianism, they could not find a mode of resistance other than force and the sword. Confrontations in the world of ideas, instead of focusing on the roots of the authoritarianism, became enmeshed in factional squabbles. . . . If a group found that the rulers protected their factional interests, they cooperated with them, and if their own interests were threatened, they fought with the rulers. . . . The last example of this was the symbiosis of senior Shiite clergy with the Safavid autocratic Shiite despots, as the former justified the latter's rule. Far less common in the history of our political thought is questioning the very nature of authoritarianism and searching for ways to overcome it.

From this general historical discussion I will now try to shed light on the problem of our own underdevelopment and why a century and half after the founding of the Dar-Alfonun, we are still on the first step. Again, transformation and progress require thought, and thought only flourishes in an atmosphere of freedom. But our history has not allowed human character to grow and to be appreciated, and thus the basic human yearning for thinking and freedom has been unattended at best and negated at worst.

In the past two hundred years we have encountered an additional problem, namely authoritarianism and dictatorship of a more dangerous and destructive character that took over our society. In this period, the hideous phenomenon of colonialism became widespread in the world, afflicting us with a colonialism-dependent dictatorship. Dictatorship no longer appeared as one power-ful tribe or nation dominating us, . . . but came in the form of an internal authoritarianism which was depen-dent on protecting the interests of a global colonist. For-eign colonist powers wanted to rob all our material and spiritual resources, propping up dictatorships as tame and complacent tools for the realization of their goals.

Unfortunately, because of what has happened to us, our temperament has not been trained to be receptive to freedom such that in the past half-century every time the ground has been ripe for us to experience freedom, we have squandered the opportunity.

In the aftermath of August 25, 1941, when an atmosphere of relative freedom came about in Iran . . . social movements became confused and incapacitated, and opportunists tried to use this freedom to monopo-lize power. Foreign hands conspired to disallow the nat-ural order of freedom to take hold in society. This state of chaos, propelled by the treachery of some camps and the conspiracy of foreigners, created a situation that eventually led to the black coup d'etat of 1953. Finally, the Islamic revolution came to our rescue, showing us the beautiful face of freedom once more.

Today, whatever supporters and critics think of this revolution, they should concede by virtue of fairness that Iran's Islamic revolution possesses two distinct character-istics. First, while in countries such as ours anti-colonial struggles have often taken a militaristic form, in our case the authoritarianism that was supported by imperialism was not overthrown by the force of guns, but by the presence of the masses and the power of discourse and enlightenment. And second, the revolution began its life with freedom, not suppression, so much so that in the first years after its victory, the revolution was even on the verge of descending into anarchy. But as despotism had become second nature to us through our dark past, we were unable to benefit from this freedom properly. Undoubtedly, the foreign hand that over the past two centuries had overtly and covertly meddled in our internal affairs, did not sit idly by, and through conspiracy and its invisible agents, prevented us from becoming acquainted with freedom in a natural way, to learn its advantages, and to grapple with its challenges.

In our universities there were groups who took up armed struggle to overthrow the government. . . . A destructive atmosphere took hold, making all parties suspicious of all others. It is natural that the revolution's leaders could not sit idly by lest the bitter experience of 1953 repeat itself. Thus, in running the country, extreme measures had to be taken to prevent a deep descent into anarchy. At the same time, the extenuating circumstances after the revolution gave some the excuse to suppress freedom as the perceived source of dislocation in society, instead of understanding the historical obstacles to freedom. They covered their closed-minded ways under the guise of religion, when in fact their religion was nothing but a series of mental and emotional habits, habits that would be questioned in an atmosphere of freedom where ideas encountered one another freely. Thus there were many who, instead of scrutinizing the roots and causes that led freedom to descend into anarchy and destruction, . . . began to oppose freedom. Willingly or not, they saw religious and national interest as being opposed to freedom. Destroying the atmosphere of peace in the name of freedom and destroying freedom in the name of religion and national interest represent two sides of the same coin, both symptomatic of the historical ailment that we suffer from due to centuries of despotic rule which has shaped our temperament to become irreconcilable with freedom. In scrutinizing the source of our problems, we cannot blame solely the government. Before that, we ourselves must learn how we can come to deserve freedom and rights. Today in universities, in our schools, and at home, we are incapable of exercising tolerance toward one another. Let us not doubt that unless we undergo an inner transformation, we cannot expect external forces to solve our problems for us. We have to understand that the experience of freedom does not come easily and that this issue has two fundamental tenets.

First, the effects of despotism have become second

nature to us. We are all individually dictator-like in our own ways, and this unfortunate condition is evident in all strata and spheres of our society. And second, we want to experience freedom in a world that is dominated by grandiose powers who think only of their own interests, interests that they view as being in conflict with the freedom of other countries, as they focus their immense political, military, informational, and economic power on protecting their interests. If the experience of freedom has encountered difficulties in countries such as ours, we should not disregard the conspiracy of outsiders.

Here we face a paradox. On the one hand growth and progress are not possible without freedom, and on the other hand freedom will not materialize and last unless society is mature and progressive. What is to be done?

I believe that if we are fair and profound in our thinking, we will reach the conclusion that freedom has priority over growth. Of course, the road to freedom and liberty is replete with danger and difficulty. Again what I mean by freedom is the freedom to think and the security to express new thinking, and instituting a protective system for the security of the free-spirited and of thinkers. More important, I think, it is practically impossible to suppress thought, but if we live in an atmosphere of freedom, thought appears in a balanced and moderate way, and rationality becomes dominant as the power to choose and the means of choice and progress become available to the people. But if freedom is absent, thoughts that will inevitably appear in the minds of thinkers will be driven underground, and may appear in violent and explosive form through the deeds of those who do not believe in thoughtful, peaceful discourse. It is necessary to explore the relationship between freedom and national security and the positive effect of the former on the latter, and the destructive effect of the lack of freedom on social stability.

The desired outcome is that the elite and thinkers reach a consensus that in today's world we must not search for a single Procrustean model of freedom for all nations. While the essence of freedom is the same, on the basis of their different social conditions and historical experiences, different nations may experience it in different ways, and choose different ways and priorities regarding the demands of freedom.

Second, let us try to create the proper atmosphere so that we can extend tolerance to one another more easily and to share each other's view of freedom, to share our minimal expectations and priorities, and to base it on the rule of law, ensuring the survival and protection of freedom. It is in such an atmosphere that our progress will be accelerated, guaranteeing a brighter future for our people. . . .

Tradition, Modernity, and Development ∾

Thinking about the meaning of the above three concepts and discerning the relationship among them is one of the most pressing preoccupations of thinkers in our age, especially in non-Western countries. A superficial glance at the above terms may lead us to conclude prematurely that modernity is a Western phenomenon, built through the dismantling and breaking of tradition. Then there is development, viewed as the upshot of modernity, which has become a paramount strategic goal of those outside the Western sphere of thought and values. From such assumptions we can reach the simplistic conclusion that to reach development it is necessary to embark on modernization, and modernization can only come about through dismantling tradition.

But these arbitrary assumptions can only satisfy the feeble-minded or those who feel no responsibility for human destiny. The problem is much too complex to be solved with simplistic solutions. Tradition cannot be transformed through mere prescriptions, nor does modernization come about easily, for, until people themselves change, no fateful transformation will happen in their lives, and the transformation of people is a highly complex affair for which individuals often lack the tools. . . .

Terms such as tradition, modernization, and development are replete with ambiguity, and thus far there is no consensus on how to define them. Indeed, consensus may never emerge. In order to minimize misunderstanding, all those engaged in this debate must specify clearly what they mean by these terms before they leap to offer their theories and prescriptions. . . .

What do I understand modernization and tradition to mean? When we talk about modernity, we are certainly talking about innovative and evolving phenomena and institutions. But are all new phenomena modern? Or does modernity mark a specific era in history? Human society, even its most primitive kinds in antiquity, has always been in flux. The essential difference between the Old World and the modern era is not in the static nature of the old versus the dynamism of the modern, but in the slow pace of change in the Old World and the breathtaking pace of change in modernity. . . .

Putting the intricate debate about the relationship between civilization and culture aside for the moment, . . . it is fair to assume that each culture is attuned and adapted to a specific civilization. Modern civilization came about through the dismantling of the previous civilization and through overturning the culture corresponding to the old civilization. Then modern civilization ushered in a culture to fit and meet its demands. . . .

Tradition, by definition, deals with the past, but we cannot think of all old things as denoting tradition. We talk about divine traditions or natural traditions which are considered constant and immutable by their proponents. . . .The laws governing existence are divine or natural traditions. It is possible that humans commit errors in the discovery of these laws, and later come to recognize their errors, but what changes here is the understanding of the laws, not the laws themselves. We may accept the principle of change and instability in the essence of the world, just as Sadr al-Mote 'allehin — among the great Muslim philosophers — believes in "dynamic essences," or just as Marxists see the world as being propelled by internal contradictions, and thus immersed in a constant state of transformation. Thus, the principle of change is permanent for everything. . . .

In my view tradition is a human affair pertaining to the mental and emotional predispositions of a people; in other words, tradition comprises the habituated thoughts, beliefs, and deeds of a people, that have been institutionalized in society on the basis of past practices.

In this definition, tradition is similar to culture, and in many instances tradition is itself a symbol of culture, but we cannot think of all culture as being traditional. Tradition is the existing culture in a society that has once possessed a compatible civilization. But now, even though the old civilization has withered, aspects of the corresponding culture have remained deeply entrenched. By civilization I do not refer only to advanced and complex civilizations, but to a specific way of life broadly defined. Thus hunter-gatherers, too, had a civilization; indeed, for as long as human society has existed, there has been civilization.

The existence of a past culture in the present while the base civilization has withered is possible because culture has roots in the depths of human beings and may be more long-lasting than the underlying civilization. Many cultural legacies may outlast civilizations by centuries. In other words, tradition is the reflection of past culture in today's life if the civilization has changed.

When a new civilization is created and the culture appropriate for it is entrenched, people who still carry around vestiges of the previous culture experience a contradiction when encountering a new civilization. On the one hand, the realities of life are affected by modern civilization, but much that contradicts modern civilization is still in place, too. People and nations like us are deeply affected by this contradiction. Most of the cultural uncertainties in our society, which has vast differences with the West, are attributable to this contradiction, which until solved at the root, will continue to spawn crisis.

Western society's embracing modern civilization came about through breaking with tradition. The beginning of modern civilization should be seen as the point when the thoughts and values of the Catholic Church and the social and economic traditions of feudalism were questioned and then rejected. The victor in this challenge was modern civilization and the leaders of this value system. The fundamentals of this system were exported to America from Europe . . . and from these two places to distant corners of the world and became dominant, even affecting life in our country.

At the same time, our past culture continues to live within us; this culture has serious differences and disagreements with Western culture. In other words, our tradition is more suitable for another civilization. That civilization no longer exists and the present civilization's border has expanded and affected us fundamentally.

As we all know, this civilization established itself by dismantling the civilization of the Middle Ages in the West. But we had a different civilization from the West in the Middle Ages. . . . Thus, even though modern civilization was at odds with the Western civilization of the Middle Ages, does this mean that the same schism exists between modernity and our previous civilization? This may have something to do with the difference between Islamic and Christian civilizations and cultures. . . .

The most important similarity of our thought today to what was dominant in the West in the Middle Ages is the central place accorded to God in the lives of humans. By contrast, in modern civilization secular humans are viewed as being the center. Even the chief architects of modern thinking — such as Descartes who emerged at the dawn of the modern era — who have defended God and the supernatural in principle, have a markedly different view than Christians and Muslims of the Middle Ages. The centrality of the role of humans constitutes the chief difference among them.

Of course, there has always been divine, mystical, and religious thinking in the West. But there is no doubt that as God and religion were central to the Middle Ages, nature and humans are central to the modern world. In the Middle Ages other-worldly issues carried more weight and prestige, and here Muslims and Christians were similar. But in today's world, focus on the afterlife has been replaced by secular concerns.

In the modern world, even though the boundless optimism of eighteenth-century Westerners has faded, science and its offspring technology are still the most important factors guiding human life. And people — at least in social spheres — do not see any reason to rely on anything other than empirical science and human perceptions. In the past, the view of humans from being and from science was different from today's. The value of knowledge was not measured by its utility in the practical affairs of this world, but by the nobility and exalted place of its subject matter. Thus, inquiry into metaphysics, and especially theology, were viewed as being the most important branches of knowledge.

In social life, it was claimed that religious law, or the apparent meaning discerned from religious texts, should rule supreme. And besides divine "revelation" humanity did not need another source for knowledge and practice . . . . It is worth mentioning that in the Muslim world, philosophy under the influence of Aristotelian and neo-Platonic views — which was essentially different from modern philosophy and rationality — was faced with statutory and canonical views of religion among the rulers and the population, and the effect of Sufism among much of the elite and some parts of society, and thus remained isolated and confined to the sidelines.

The beginning of the modern age can be seen as a time when the main measure of the significance of knowledge and science became their practical utility in this world, whereas before then, the dominant thinking had rested on the folly of the physical world. And even though Muslims of that time were ahead of their Christian contemporaries in recognizing the validity — and indeed the significance — of the natural and physical world, in both civilizations focusing on the natural world was viewed as being a largely futile occupation.

The crux of my argument is that today's civilization dominates us non-Westerners as well, and that this civilization requires a culture that is attuned to it. Yet portions of our culture remains attuned to a bygone civilization. Modern civilization was built through the dismantling of the previous civilization and the accompanying culture.

Thus we must concede that the incompatibility of modern civilization with our tradition-bound civilization is one of the most important causes of the crisis in our society. What is to be done? Should we insist on remaining immersed in our tradition, or should we melt fully into Western civilization? Or is there another way of removing this contradiction, or at least taming and channeling it such that it does not lead to our destruction and the unraveling of our social fabric and historical identity? . . .

Many traditionalists continue to defend their heritage against modernity, often thinking of this heritage as being divine, assuming that they can bring order to their lives by shutting the doors to Western values and civilization, and by relying on tradition. But this ill-fated rigidity has not achieved their aims, a fact evident in Western civilization's success in exporting much of its values to unprepared tradition-bound societies that have lacked the capability to understand the West. Thus, traditionalists have been left with no choice but to retreat progressively, without providing society with the tools to appraise Western civilization properly. . . .

Then there are those who believe that this crisis can be solved by a complete and uncritical adopting of modern values. Modernity, to them, counts as the highest achievement of humankind to date as they prescribe that all obstacles for its embrace be removed, tradition being viewed the biggest obstacle in the process of modernization. They advise that we prepare the way for the new civilization by stepping on our past heritage. But sadly, many who have been entranced by the admittedly awesome accomplishments of the West, those who have represented the essence of what became known in our society as intellectualism, have not only not solved the problem, but made it worse.

First, the shallowness of their view, the debate being merely glossed over, has postponed the emergence of a real debate about the relationship between modernity and tradition. Second, dispensing with deeply rooted traditions, they have proved incapable of achieving any-thing of significance. They have never found a place in the hearts of a people who have become habituated to tradition; they have not spoken a language comprehensi-ble to the people, and thus have died in isolation, their words never gaining common currency. Or even worse, in order to survive they wrapped themselves around autocratic rulers, often becoming the tools of Western colonialism in their own countries.

In real life, neither religious decrees and mere wishful thinking can prevent the advance of Western culture, nor can memoranda and doctrines uproot tradition. Human life is always changing, sometimes unconsciously and uncontrollably. The important thing is to see through which perspective we can maintain an instrumen-tal presence in the process of change, so that instead of being at their mercy, we can confront circumstances with awareness and intelligence.

Alongside these two imagined solutions, there are reform-minded thinkers in the developing world. While there is hope that this movement may be more successful, thus far it, too, has been beleaguered by the crisis that we face. This is because reformists rest on two fundamen-tals: One, a return to the self and reviving our historical-cultural identity, and two, a positive encounter with the achievements of human civilization, while being aware of the hegemonic and colonial legacy of the West. Not only is there no unity of vision about the "self" that they want to return to, but also they cannot agree on precisely those aspects of the West that we must absorb and internalize. . . . Thus reformists must be viewed as keen and aware pioneers who have tried to confront their society's woes courageously to rid it of degrading conditions. . . .

Our past has been eventful, but our future remains uncertain. We are adrift in a world dominated by Western culture, politics, economics, and military might, and confront the idea of development which is a tested form of progress in the West. And we must decide once and for all where we stand in relation to the West and how Western values are related to development, so that we can attain development without losing our national identity or becoming dissolved in the West. . . .

Development, like many other contemporary concepts, has its roots in the West. Here is how I define it: to establish widespread welfare on the basis of the values and criteria of Western civilization. Don't we divide the world into the two camps of "developed" — meaning built on Western values — and "undeveloped?" Don't we think of those countries as "developing" that are trying to modernize their way of life by emulating the West? It is here that the relationship between tradition and modernity comes into focus.

Development is a Western concept, based on Western civilization, . . . Without knowing it we cannot know development, let alone make decisions about it or reject it. . . . So, I believe that debating about development is premature before focusing on its underpinnings.

There are those who claim that nations are doomed to remain backward, even to perish, unless they meet all of development's demands. And modernization, they say, is necessary to achieve development.

The above judgment is true if we see the West as the ultimate human civilization that is impossible to supersede in the future, but there are those who see the West as the latest but not the ultimate human civilization, which like all other human artifacts, is tentative and susceptible to decay. Of course, this does not mean denying development or surrendering to the views of regressive traditionalists; it means rejecting the prescriptions of those who prescribe complete and rapid Westernization. While the prescriptions of thinkers usually differ from those of the power elite, development will be achieved more fully if policy making is attuned to the prescriptions of rational thought, not itself a constraint on thinking.

Our role as thinkers is to realize that even if development means repeating the Western experience, we still have to fathom its basic tenets and their implications. This represents the most important calling for real intellectualism and thinking. The truth of the matter is that without rationality real development will be impossible to attain.

First, development is not a mechanical process that can be achieved in the absence of rational human beings. And second, a society that is devoid of rational thinking will lose its balance as soon as it encounters problems, and it is amply clear that human difficulties cannot be solved through reliance on force, strict laws, and the decrees of politicians, even though difficulties might be submerged by these means for a while. . . .

The sad experience of the Westoxicated and the tradition-bound is before us, and we must learn from their mistakes so we do not repeat them.

Modern civilization is the important reality of our age and has brought many monumental benefits to humanity. But its faults are many as well, and these faults are not limited to Westerners' political and economic atrocities outside their geographic borders. The West faces serious internal crises in its economy, society, and in its thinking. For those of us living outside the West, if we don't feel overwhelmed and taken in by the West, we will at least be better judges of the disasters brought about by Western colonialism for non-Westerners. . . .

Western civilization is a human construct, and thus tentative and prone to decay, unless someone claims unrealistically that with the dawn of modern civilization, the fountain of human curiosity and creativity has dried up. Civilization is an answer to the curiosity of humans who never stop questioning their world. The ever-changing needs of humans compel them to fulfill these needs, and civilization is the answer to the questions one faces. Of course, there are important questions and needs in history that spur the emergence of civilizations, and these questions are themselves affected by the time and place in which they arise. . . . That is why civilizations change and there is no such thing as an ultimate and eternal civilization. For as long as there are humans, so will be their curiosity and needs. With each question that is answered and each need that is fulfilled, humans are confronted with new questions and needs. . . .

Each civilization remains standing until it can harness its inner power to offer answers to human questions and to fulfill human needs, but civilization, similar to all secular things, is limited. When it depletes its natural strength and cannot find answers to new questions, slowly the exuberance of followers of this civilization will vanish, and that is how civilizations decay and perish.

Western civilization has encountered great crises, and by relying on its natural strengths, it has been able to pass through them beginning in the nineteenth century and culminating in the two world wars of this century. But the liberal and capitalist West managed to confront and outlive its socialist opponent through adjusting its institutions. Precipitated by its own internal weaknesses, socialism's demise dazzled the world. It is nonetheless clear that the West is faced with other deep crises, crises that have arisen out of questioning the core values of the West evident in a decrease in confidence in its capabilities and permanence. These questions are now more pressing and pertinent than ever. Thus, objections to the moral and philosophical bases of the West are more common today. . . .

It is true that the inability of the culture of the Middle Ages to offer answers to human curiosity and needs, and resorting to physical and psychological force to suppress those questions and needs, led to an intellectual and social explosion which caused the rule of the Church and feudal overlords to crumble. But it would be naïve to think of these conscious questions and needs as the sole cause of the emergence of modern civilization. These questions and needs emerged amid motivations which were outside the realm of logic and rationality. . . .

First, the harsh restrictions imposed by the Church and feudalism were instrumental in bringing about a reaction in the opposite direction. The Church had given its practices a sacred façade such that its excesses led Westerners not only to overturn the extant social order, but to doubt the whole validity of religion and spirituality.

At the same time, hedonism and greed played a great role in the birth and rise of modern civilization, which has trampled on higher truths and spirituality.

Was the role of the bourgeoisie any less significant to the development of modernity than that of the intellectual founders of the movement? What drove the bourgeois class was certainly not a restless search for truth and justice, and the rescue of these two ends from the excesses of the Church and feudalism, but the will to acquire wealth.

Liberty, brotherhood, and egalitarianism were the key promises of the French revolution, but these promises were themselves tools in the hands of the new bourgeois class as it competed with the aristocracy for power, driven by the boundless ambition that characterized the new-rich. It is even possible to claim that the scientists and intellectuals of modernity were actually providing rational and intellectual justification for the wants and ambitions of the new class. As we praise the many achievements of Western civilization such as modern science, technology, freedom of thought, and democracy, we cannot overlook the colonialism, the use of deadly force against non-Westerners, the plunder of other peoples' material and cultural riches, polluting the earth's environment, perpetuating half-truths and lies, and the opportunism that also characterize the West. . . .

Thus we cannot surrender to all that is Western . . . . At the same time we cannot deal with tradition superficially; tradition is the essence of the sociohistorical achievements of a people, especially important to us since we have had a rich culture and history. . . . As Aristotle says in his *Politics,* habit and tradition play an important role in keeping a good society together.

Breaking with tradition means destroying the cultural and historical heritage of a people, but if a people are to evolve they must understand their past to see where they are in their process of historical evolution. Thus, dismantling aspects of tradition must be based on indigenous models, not imported and artificial. Indeed, Westerners at the dawn of modernity were awakened by delving deeply into their tradition. Thinkers revisited the artistic tradition of the Greeks and the social traditions of Rome. Religious believers returned to what they considered to be the most authentic aspects of Christianity, and hence the Reformation. And these returns to tradition and reappraisals ushered in the new epoch. . . .

In such a world, the bourgeoisie, aided by secular thinkers, achieved victory on the basis of the new thinking which rested on a return to previous ways of rational thinking. . . . Thus, even in the effort to dismantle tradition, there is no escaping tradition.

We who have the will to evolve, and who want to

take the reigns of destiny into our hands to be able to transform it, must ensure that our seeking of Western models of development does not lead to destroying our heritage. We can only critique tradition if we have a firm sense of our own identity; a traditionless people are invariably devoid of serious thought. Weak-willed and brittle, they are at the mercy of events.

This aside, there is the practical problem that tradition is too deeply rooted in human life to be dismantled by the mere decree of politicians or prescriptions of intellectuals, Even worse, forcing this process may actually exacerbate problems and rob society of identity. But this is not the same as surrendering to tradition unconditionally. . . .

Tradition, much like civilization, is a human construct and susceptible to change. The continuous transformation of traditions at varying speeds all over history is ultimate proof that further change is inevitable. The important issue is to what extent the process of change is initiated consciously with maximum participation of the people themselves, instead of being handed down from above or being forced upon people by circumstance. . . .

Traditions are bound to evolve. The question remains whether or not people should ever be forced to maintain traditions in spite of needs, desires, and requirements of the human way of life. . . .

Tradition, Modernity, and Development

Tradition is dependent on the understanding and intuition of people, who are themselves prone to change. This change does not negate the existence of all absolutes, but merely necessitates the recognition that our interpretations of the absolute change over time. Has human understanding of the divine been constant over history?

The important point is that as interpretations get entrenched, as they sink into the historical memory of a people and society, turning away from them becomes difficult, and this difficulty is exacerbated when traditions adopt the veneer of sanctity such that any criticism or objection directed at these habits and interpretations is viewed as sacrilege. Combating sacrilege is a divine duty, making this problem more acute in religious societies.

It is certain that our thinking and lifestyles need transformation. Much of the time, tradition is the greatest obstacle to development, unless we actively participate in transforming and reconstructing it.

Our society needs to evolve and transform itself, but we must know that development in its Western sense is merely one form of transformation, not the only form. Development in the West is the upshot of reliance on tradition and deep historical understanding which paved the way for a new understanding of humans and being among Westerners.

Westerners have been through a difficult and long process. Only after passing through many vicissitudes have they achieved rational wisdom and will. The search for truth, as well as competition, vindictiveness, and ambition have all combined to make modernity and development appear.

We live in a time when the inner weaknesses of the West are becoming evident not only to those outside the West, but to Westerners themselves, who now doubt their noble manifest destiny. Awareness of this issue compels us to refrain from buying fully into Western notions of development. At the same time, we cannot view tradition as being immutable and divine either.

Therefore, we face two human challenges, one deeply rooted in our society, the other imported and in some instances dominant over us, namely modern civilization. The important thing is to not defy either of these, as some have done. . . .

For understanding today, we must know the demands of tomorrow, and for properly understanding the future we have no choice but to acquaint ourselves with our history. Tomorrow is a time when humanity transcends today's civilization, and those who get there sooner will be those who are familiar with the past and focus on the future, not the rigidly tradition-bound, nor the superficially modern who understand only the façade of today's civilization.

Why not focus on the coming civilization, and adjust all transformations to fit that ideal. Such an ambitious plan requires that we critique both modernity and tradition.

Of course, entering the future does not imply dismantling today. Only those who reach a level of growth, awareness and courage to be able to incorporate all the achievements of humankind can build a new epoch and become masters of tomorrow.

We are by no means doomed to dissolve into modern civilization, but we cannot ignore its many great scientific, social, and political achievements. Why can't we transcend today to establish a new relationship to existence and achieve a new vision, and in its shadow become the source of a new civilization which, while resting on our historical identity, and benefiting from the accomplishment of modern civilization, could inaugurate a new chapter in human life. This is especially promising to us Iranians and Muslims who have a record of creating civilizations that have played a central role in human history. Why can't we be the originator of civilization again? Of course this does not mean that we should return to the past to stay there — which would be regressive — but that we must find a secure launching ground to move beyond the present and toward a future that is dependent on our present and our past.

Reason and Religion ⌒୬

Matters such as the place of religion in our age, the role of people in shaping their destiny, the relationship between religion and modernity and religious government to liberalism, as well as the relationship between religion and democracy, are central issues for us today. If we do not attend to them, it will only be we who are absent from the scene. A person truly living in his own time is one who understands today's world and tries to offer more innovative solutions to current problems. If we are present physically in time but absent in thought, we cannot claim to be present in our own time. Today, friends of our revolution wish to know what models and plans this revolution offers for life, and foes hope that this revolution fails and fades from the scene. Thus, these are pressing issues present in our time that must be addressed. . . .

Three great historical figures — Imam Khomeini, and martyrs Motahhari and Sadr — have played an important role in our recent history and in shaping the thinking of the current age, especially among new generations of Muslims. Their greatest achievement was their ability to transform the Muslim world culturally, especially Shiism. Imam Khomeini, who was the harbinger of new thinking and a new culture, became the source of a great historical transformation. These three were exceptional in their knowledge and experience and no thinker and scholar can ignore or circumvent their insights. For those without formal religious training, heeding the prescriptions of the clergy is necessary in practical matters, but in the realm of thought, no thinker can blindly follow the clergy, however outstanding they are — unless religious leaders are among the Infallibles. That is why I do not believe that great figures such as Motahhari and Sadr had the last word in religious and intellectual matters.

The point to focus on is that these were pioneers who took the first steps with confidence, and in this sense represent models for us to emulate. They are indeed worthy of tremendous respect. But their ideas must be subjected to critique. Did Motahhari and Sadr bring a new discourse to our society? I believe that the new discourse had already begun to permeate our society before the involvement of these figures, arising from our encounter with the West. Some rigidly traditional parts of our society completely rejected the West, while some

Westernized intellectuals sought to dissolve themselves in the West. And there were reformers of religious thought in the Sunni and Shiite sects of Islam such as Seyyed Jamal-Eddin Assadabadi, Sheikh Mohammad Abdeh, Ighbal Lahouri, Allameh Naeeni, and great figures such as Motahhari, Shariati and Sadr who wanted neither to dissolve into the West, nor to completely reject it, hoping instead to chart a healthy middle ground. A book by Assadabadi, for example, put forth a critique of materialism that generated lengthy discourse in this tradition.

Before the time of martyrs Motahhari and Sadr, Allameh Tabatabai in Iran and many thinkers elsewhere in the Muslim world had tried to find new answers to these types of questions. What makes Mottahari and Sadr exceptional is their attempt to defend Islamic thought from Marxist and materialist thought so as to be able to usher in a new discourse based on a deep understanding of issues. This discourse must be the focus of all clerics and intellectuals who believe in religion and enlightenment.

The question of the West's deficiencies needs more precise scrutiny. Major differences exist between our religious thought and Western values. Our thinking is based on the existence of an omnipotent, all-knowing God, while the West rejects such a being, at least in the sphere of running social affairs. This is a great difference between us which implies that in spiritual matters the West has less power than we do.

At present the West possesses economic, technological and scientific power, while we Muslims lag behind in this area. The *Qur'an* prescribes, "Against them make ready your strength to the utmost of your power" *(Holy Qur'an,* 9.60) in effect counseling us to attain the material sources of power as well, such that we can demand our rights on the basis of this power. It is here that I want to distinguish foundations from guidelines, for I see civilization as a foundation, not a guiding light. Civilization is built upon the specific beliefs, needs, and concerns of people. As such a people's beliefs may change and so may civilization. After the Prophet Mohammad, in the third and fourth Muslim centuries (8th and 9th centuries C.E.), Muslims created a new civilization on the basis of the teachings of Islam, the *Qur'an,* and what they had learned from Persian and Greek civilizations. But the fact that the golden age of Islamic civilization has passed does not mean that the *Qur'an* and Islam have withered too. We Muslims believe that we must maintain our faith in the *Qur'an* and authentic Islam while searching for new answers to today's questions on the basis of religion. The products of Western civilization are everywhere, but I believe that this civilization, too, is not ultimate because it is a human construct.

All human achievements must be utilized by new generations, just as Western civilization borrowed heavily from the Islamic world, which in turn had been enriched in its golden age by Persian and Greek culture. My main question is, what should we Muslims do now that Western civilization is dominant and we have lost our previous civilization? If we want to be instrumental in today's world, should we return to the West's past — which would be regressive — or do we want to transcend Western civilization, or do we merely want to dissolve into the West?

The rigidly traditional want us to return to the past. The Westernized prescribe that we melt into the West, but those who really care about the well-being of their national and religious culture believe that we must incorporate the West to be able to transcend it, remaining aware of our own religious sources, as well as the questions and puzzles of today's world. We must adopt all of the positive achievements of the West, but see them in relation to our own heritage so we can fill in its deficiencies. That is why we must place greater focus on the future of the West than on its past.

Rectitude is one of the pillars of all religions, especially Islam, and we need a specific interpretation of the term. Unfortunately the idea of rectitude in the history of Islam has been limited to the realm of the individual, because the truly pious of the Shiite faith have never governed society.

This has also been true of the Sunnis; the only people who were allowed to govern were the powerful, while the people were kept away from the reigns of power. Social rectitude has no precedent in our history. The same Muslims who believed in rectitude committed many social injustices in the Muslim world, and individual rectitude has not been able to overturn these inequities.

Thus if we say that we possess rectitude and the West does not, we have to know exactly what we mean by rectitude. To religious believers, the relationship between God and humans is clear, but the relationship of subjects to their rulers, individuals to their society, and various constituents of society to one another have not been scrutinized deeply enough to enable us to know the requirements of this-worldly rectitude.

Westerners believe that their culture is based on liberty. Before the advent of modern civilization, the issues of social, political, and civil liberties did not exist in the West because pre-modern Muslims and Westerners of the Middle Ages believed in salvation. Today, salvation is conceived as living free of restrictions, but in the Old World it meant freedom from internal restrictions and deficiencies such as worldly lust.

Some sects in the Islamic world went so far as saying that salvation can only come from self-denial and shunning all material objects, including even society. Farabi viewed Sufis, who prescribed such denial, as ignorant. He believed in salvation, too, but he felt that salvation can only come through immersion in a civil society guided by freedom from internal restraints and defects. But liberty, as conceived in the West, is the exact opposite of this because it rests on freedom from external intrusions into one's life, such that one's life is governed by no one other than one's self. The Western idea of individualism gives primacy to human understanding and desires, and a free person is one whose search for the fulfillment of needs is not hindered by anything. Of course liberty has limits and that is the liberty of others. This liberty has also had positive effects as people have taken their destiny into their own hands, and government has become a servant of the people and accountable to them, not their master. In contrast, in previous autocratic regimes, rulers were above the people and thought of them as mere pawns at the complete mercy of their rulers. But when people were freed from the shackles of this domination, they collectively gained power over their rulers.

Liberty is freedom from external bonds. In contrast, the pre-modern idea of salvation rested on freedom from inner bonds, oblivious to social and political liberties and rights. Both of these visions are incomplete. Modern liberalism ignores internal freedom, and while it is not concerned with whether or not humans are slaves to their passions, it requires that humans not be subjugated by the whims of their rulers. We, on the contrary, have tried to prevent people from falling prey to their desires, even though tyrants governed and enchained Muslim society. My prescription is that we try to attain both kinds of freedom, as we refer to the *Qur'an* and our society. We may reject many aspects of Western liberalism, but we cannot deny its many achievements. As we discern the faults and strong points of the West, we must also direct this form of critical thinking at ourselves.

Reason can be defined in various ways, and we must specify what kind of reason we mean: Platonic, Aristotelian, neo-Platonic, the reason envisioned by Muslims and the Sufis, the reason of Ibn-Roshd, or that of Descartes, Kant, or Hegel.

In my view, reason is the common bond of all humans, a means of connecting to the world and to others, the same reason through which Plato and Aristotle communicated their views. Reason and intellect represent the only way of understanding this world, even though this understanding is too relative to guide us to ultimate truths. Our great thinkers, while aware of the indispensability of reason, knew that reason alone could not discover all of reality. Our religious tradition claims that it is ultimately faith of the heart, not the intellect, that comprehends the whole of reality.

If we think of reason and faith as contradictory and opposed to one another, because reason achieves more instrumental impact in this world, faith will be sidelined. It is important to note that the faith I am talking about exists alongside and parallel to reason, not in opposition to it.

Reason can merely take us to the gates of the afterlife. Even though it is aware that the world is not limited to the material, it cannot go farther than this world. It is here that faith must step in. Humans cannot do without reason in their lives as they encounter practical matters, and if they have to choose between faith and reason, they will choose the latter. Interpretations of the world based on reason are relative, a relativity that also permeates our perceptions of religion. But if our understanding of religious tradition and the *Qur'an* gets moribund and in need of transformation, this does not mean that tradition and the *Qur'an* have aged themselves. Our intellect is capable of adapting to the current world while also remaining attuned to tradition and the *Qur'an* such that the solid essence of religion is not harmed. Our religious thinking is bound to evolve.

Humans instinctively seek God, a reality present in the direct experiential contact with the divine. Unfortunately, many of our anachronistic interpretations of religion have assumed the veneer of sanctity and are viewed as being immutable.

It is certain that humans will take further steps toward spiritual fulfillment, for a narrow and materialistic existence will inevitably torment them. We believe that religion does not oppose material well being, but invites all humans to a grander, more exalted place than the material world.

As a believer I am certain that the future belongs to religion; as an advocate of reason, I can already see the signs of the eager reception awaiting religion in today's world.

Our Revolution and the Future of Islam ❦

Civilizations rise and fall. From the dawn of history this has been the fate of Sumerian, Chaldean, Assyrian, Chinese, Indian, Persian, Greek, Roman, and Islamic civilizations. At its zenith, Islam acted as the conduit between these ancient civilizations and the modern age. Today, it is Western civilization that reigns supreme, casting its shadow upon all corners of the world.

The Interplay of Civilizations

Unless they are completely unaware of each other's existence, civilizations ordinarily affect and transform one another. For instance, America's indigenous civilization was completely unknown to the outside world until Europeans discovered the continent. But once the connection was made, the massive tide of explorers and immigrants who conquered and appropriated the new world could not be held back. Using their superior power and resources, the newcomers ruthlessly subjugated and destroyed the continent's old civilization. The wave of European immigrants that took over the Americas eventually succeeded in turning North America into the most powerful center of Western civilization.

Give-and-take among civilizations is the norm of history. Prior to the discovery of the Americas, the civilizations of Asia, Africa, and Europe had been in contact since antiquity, transforming one another in various ways. Fundamentally influenced by Greek civilization, Islam played a central mediating role by introducing Europeans to the achievements of Greek thought and philosophy. Thus "new" civilizations are never new in the true sense, for they always feed on the work of previous civilizations, appropriating and digesting all that fits their needs, dispensing with all that does not.

The Main Sources of the Emergence of Civilizations

Of the many factors that spur the emergence, rise, and demise of civilizations, two are fundamental: the dynamism of the human mind and the concomitant surfacing of new needs and necessities in human life.

The human mind is instinctively active, perpetually driven by a burning curiosity that confronts a never-ending chain of new questions to which it must find answers, or it will not rest or be content. But once a discovery is made, the new answers bring to view an untested world replete with new questions, an eternal cyclical process.

At the same time, humans strive to fulfill their material needs, which beckons them to seek greater mastery over the natural world through invention and innovation. The combination of the will to dominate nature and the will to create alters the material and psychological makeup of the human world, and this creates new needs and necessities.

The dynamism of the human constitution and the resulting search for answers to pressing questions or needs spurs a constant transformation of the human historical consciousness. And the same two fundamental qualities of humans that underpin the inevitability of change are also the cause of the emergence and decline of civilizations. While other human, social, and natural factors slow down or accelerate the coming, going, and interchange of civilizations, the desire and need for change is the most important in this regard.

Every civilization is based on a specific world-view which is itself shaped by a people's idiosyncratic historical experience. For as long as the existing world view successfully addresses the fundamental questions and needs of a community, it remains intact. But when the collective consciousness and soul of a people outgrows the limitations of the existing civilization, the search for new ideas begins in earnest, often taking the form of turning to other civilizations for clues. This is the secret of the emergence, flourishing, and fall of all civilizations.

The Crisis of Civilizations

When it is first born and subsequently at the point of its demise, each civilization places its adherents in a state of crisis. At first, when a new covenant arises in the history of a people and the ground is ripe for the emergence of a new civilization, the social fabric is strained. The new civilization heralds new and often revolutionary customs and mores. But the previous civilization will not easily relinquish its entrenched and institutionalized dominance. Historically shaped social habits are hard to break. Much of society remains glued to the mental and emotional predilections of the previous era. The need to throw out the deeply ingrained attachments and replace them with a new world view induces a painful identity crisis.

At the same time, the new civilization has not been tried out in real life. Its inner contradictions are hidden from view, for it has not passed the litmus test of experience. To endure and lay roots, the new civilization must adapt and fine-tune itself as it encounters the evolving realities of social life. Until this process of adaptation and transformation reaches its fruition, social identity crisis is the norm.

The other instance of crisis, at the point of the demise of a civilization, appears when the dominant world view cannot satisfy the psychological, material, and social needs of its constituents. People begin to experience a troubling void and sterility. Again, the historically conditioned predilections that are rendered anachronistic will not be easily abandoned. This state of limbo can merely offer the veneer of civilization bereft of substance and soul. An existential void sets in that brings on a full-blown identity crisis.[1]

This discussion is meant to set up the fundamental question, what historical condition does our own society live in and what is going to become of it?

Crisis in the West

Indeed, ours is the age of the dominance and entrenchment of Western civilization, a civilization that has lived for more than four centuries and has made great strides in science, politics, and social regulation. But we must accept that the West today faces an acute crisis, a crisis in its thought and all other spheres. Those familiar with the history of Western civilization and its philosophical, scientific, and artistic expressions can more or less see the signs of this crisis. The West was not confronted with a crisis of this magnitude in the eighteenth and part of the nineteenth century. What does the current crisis signify?

It is possible to assert that Western civilization is worn out and senile. Four centuries is a long time for a civilization — even though it is possible that in the past some civilizations may have lived longer than this. But science, technology, and electronic communication have vastly accelerated the pace of change like never before. The life of Western civilization from the Renaissance to the present cannot be viewed as short, and to treat Western civilization as old would not be an exaggeration.

From Crisis to Demise of the West?

This is not an easy question to take on. Crises are sometimes limited and temporary. This has often occurred in the life of civilizations which have displayed the ability to confront crises successfully and remain intact. For example, in the nineteenth century, the West managed to successfully surmount the crisis that it encountered.

The capitalist order, which represents a key feature of Western civilization, encountered great difficulties in the second half of the nineteenth century and during the two world wars of the first half of the twentieth century. But Marxism came to its rescue. The West managed to modify its mental and material structures, coming out of these crises in one piece.

Despite the claims of its protagonists, Marxism was an impractical and unrealistic philosophy. And precisely because of these deficiencies and its lack of adaptability, it did not last. It was kept standing for seventy years only through the use of force and propaganda. Still, although Marx did not offer a solid and comprehensive philosophy, he was a great pathologist of the capitalist order. What Marxists proposed forced the West to become introspective and to search for ways of adjusting capitalism's methods to the demands of the time, and to modify its social, economic, and political order from within. One key tactic of the West was to replace its old colonialism — which was sowing the seeds of a worldwide explosion — with neocolonialism. This allowed the West to contain and diffuse the crisis, postponing its re-emergence for a while.

But what about the present crisis? Can the West also pass through this difficult period unscathed? We cannot predict this with certainty, but to the extent that human understanding and research allows, we can collect evidence and observe empirical reality and arrive at a theory on that basis. This is an important task for objective and judicious academic research.

The West's Antidotes for Crisis

The West has adopted a strategy similar to the one it used at the beginning of this century which allowed it to circumvent previous crises: by modifying the ways of old colonialism into a more sophisticated neocolonialism. The so-called "new world order" is the West's new strategy for handling a crisis that has shaken it at the core.

Presenting itself as the main sponsor and protector of the "new world order," the United States is focused on adapting neocolonialism[2] to the new age. The logic of this transformation is similar to the shift from old colonialism to neocolonialism. There is other evidence attesting to the decline of the current Western civilization as well. While it is certain that Western civilization is old and worn out, the question of whether it has reached the end of its path needs more thinking and scrutiny. What does the future hold?

Crisis in Our Revolutionary Society

Our society also confronts a crisis today, and although this crisis is to some extent attributable to global conditions, it is different from the West's crisis. Through our revolution we tried to free ourselves from the shackles of the West's domination. Our revolution made us introspective, we decided to struggle for our independence, to be masters of our own fate. In this regard, we have made great headway in the political, economic, and cultural spheres. But is it possible that we fall into the West's trap of domination again? This depends on the path we choose in the future and on what the West's own destiny is. The Islamic revolution was a momentous event in the history of the Iranian nation and the Islamic community, and we can rightly say that because of our revolution we have dispensed with many borrowed and Western values that dominated our thinking. And through realizing our own authentic historical and cultural identity, we have laid a completely new groundwork for regulating our society.

Our revolution proposed the creation of a religiously based system and our society accepted this with enthusiasm and took steps to reach this great goal. The crisis that we experience today can only be remedied if we shed the vestiges of our borrowed identity and don a new garb. Our current crisis is the crisis of birth which I referred to earlier. Our new civilization is on the verge of emergence.

We cannot confront this crisis with trepidation. We must embrace it boldly and intelligently. Only when we have understood the most fundamental historical questions of this epoch can we develop the willingness to solve them.

We wish to base our life on the tenets of Islam; we possess the will to create an Islamic civilization. At a time when Western civilization is going through its last days, or at least experiencing senility, we must ask, didn't Islamic civilization already emerge once and end centuries ago? And doesn't the death of a civilization mean that we can no longer base thought and action on its teachings? Doesn't this rule apply to our history? Does the coming and passing of Islamic civilization mean that the period of Islam, which provided the basis for Islamic civilization, is over?

If the answer to this question is affirmative, has our revolution been a fruitless effort moving against the traditions of creation and laws that govern the march of civilizations? This is one of the most important and pressing questions that confronts our revolution. If we do not approach it with level-headedness and objectivity, if we cannot find a solid answer to this question, our revolution will inevitably encounter great danger and difficulty.

My answer to the above question is negative. But with this answer I do not want to debunk the rule that I proposed about civilizations. Generally, I believe that the law holds, but on the basis of my view of religion, I take this case not as a falsifier of the above but as falling outside its purview. For what creates a civilization is the vision and effort of humans, while religion is above and beyond the vision of individuals and societies and thus transcends civilizations.

If the sun has set on Islamic civilization despite its many monumental achievements, a certain view of religion — which was appropriate for that period — has ended, not the age of religion itself.

One of the greatest difficulties that religions have encountered historically has arisen out of confusing the specific religious teachings designed for specific times and places with the idea of religion itself. Naturally, with the obsolescence of age- and place-specific religious thought, some have the impression that the era of religion is over as well. But religion transcends the specific civilizations that it gives rise to.

Civilization addresses specific needs and dilemmas of a community in a particular time and place. When conditions and times change, new questions arise that in turn require new answers — and hence a new civilization.

Religion, on the other hand, sheds light on questions of eternity, charting a general and timeless path for humanity, giving direction to life despite its ever changing circumstances. Religion guides human talents to their plateau, instilling in people a sense of duty in different historical conditions.

Thus if we think of religion as being identical to civilization or culture, then the passing of civilization must imply that the era of religion is over as well. But if we believe that religion supersedes and transcends civilization and the specific mores of community, then religion can contain many different interpretations that give rise to various civilizations. The inevitable transformations of human life will do no damage to the eternal life of religion.

In this view, the core of religion possesses such

dynamism that in any age it can provide answers to questions and a fulfillment of needs. Thus, while the old Islamic civilization has vanished, religion stands deeply rooted and can generate new civilizations, even though the specific interpretations of religion which have spawned past Islamic civilizations have withered.

With this general picture, I will try to address a number of pressing issues that confront our society today.

Our vision of consolidating a system of religious governance in our future-oriented society cannot be materialized in a vacuum. We cannot implement this vision without full contact with the international community. We have come upon this important task at a time when Western civilization dominates the world. Yet simultaneously we must try to free ourselves from the domination of the West. It is thus natural that we confront the West, and the upshot of this confrontation will determine our future.

Two Countenances of the West

The West displays two features: one political, the other intellectual. Its political orientation serves as the most outward manifestation or veneer of Western civilization. The intellectual foundations of Western civilization illustrate its general world view. We must diligently distinguish between these two aspects. Only then can we find the proper way of confronting the West. This path must be traveled with prudence.

Even though the West has gotten old, it maintains tremendous political, economic, military, and technological power, simultaneously wielding a formidable propaganda and communication apparatus to manage the world's perceptions. Equally important, the global economy is controlled and regulated by Western financial institutions.

The West's advanced systems and institutions often legitimize its political power, ensuring its decisive presence in all significant global developments. The military might of Western capitalism is also vast, and even if we concede that official military pacts are not as common as they were, the military and destructive power of the West remains intact.

Politically, the West aims to govern all corners of the world and to dominate the theory and practice of international relations. It possesses the material and symbolic sources of power simultaneously, and it will stop at nothing to achieve its goals and protect its interests. Our struggle with the West is of life-and-death importance.

In its political embodiment, the West does not wish us — or any people — to be independent, free, and masters of our own fate. For if one feature of Western imperialism is violating others' territories and exploiting their economies, the concomitant feature is dominating the world of ideas. The West propagates a world view that lures its preys into subjugation.

We confront a determined enemy that brings all of its material, military, and informational resources to convince us to surrender, or risk being destroyed if we resist. The bitter experience of confrontation between domination-seeking powers and the oppressed masses is too evident to be hidden to anyone.

In political confrontations the enemy uses the mask of science and culture to deceive us. But in reality its only wish is to induce a people to surrender to its wishes and serve its interests, and to appropriate all of the victims' resources to serve the imperialist power.

Although the West has no qualms about using the most repressive and violent techniques, even its military and overtly oppressive measures are shrouded in seemingly humanistic and misleading guises that divert public opinion from reality.

When colonial powers violate other peoples, they never concede that their aim is to rob the victims' resources or to subjugate them politically. Instead, by abusing their persuasive powers they try to disguise their crimes through words and ideas that are acceptable to all of humanity. From old times, colonial powers have used the excuse of developing and civilizing other peoples to violate them and rape their lands. Today, like before, the political motto of the West remains defending freedom, human rights, and democracy.

At this juncture our struggle against the West is central to our survival. Any form of reconciliation and appeasement, given the penchant of the opponent for deception, will lead to nothing but our debasement and trampling on our pride. We must struggle against this with all our might, and victory is not beyond our reach. We must depend on God and ask for His guidance, relying on our own historical identity which we have regained through our revolution. With faith in the power of an awakened people and by strengthening the desire for independence and freedom, we must stand firmly opposed to an enemy that lacks humanitarian incentives. This is indeed possible. The awesome resistance of our nation to the conspiracies and crimes of the oppressors can be a lesson for all nations who wish to regain their independence and pride.

Yet, while ignoring the politically treacherous goals and conspiracies of the West can be catastrophic, we cannot see the West merely in political terms or reduce its whole civilization to political issues. This would also lead us to a harmful dead end.

Western civilization is not limited to its political aspects. Alongside Western politics, there is a system of

values and thinking which we must also come to understand and learn to deal with. Here we are confronted
with our philosophical and moral opposite, not just with
a political rival. To understand the West, the best tool is
rationality, not heated, flag-waving emotionalism. Not
just here, but nowhere can force offer an effective
response to a way of thinking that we consider flawed.
That would be self-defeating and counterproductive.

However, mired as they are in shallowness and hype,
it is possible that opportunists will take any thought and
culture that their audience dislikes and give it political
salience and call it a conspiracy to destroy their political
base. This does not come from contemplation but from
the need to justify their irrational encounter with opposite
views, obviating the need for education and a more powerful logic. This is very common among the overly
politicized.

Resorting to force is appropriate in confronting a
military invasion, conspiracy, or political sabotage. But
the way to oppose thought and culture is not through
the use of military, security, and judicial means, for using
force only adds fuel to the opposite side's fire. We must
confront the thought of the opponent by relying on
rationality and enlightenment and through offering
more powerful and compelling counter arguments. Only
comprehensive and attractive thinking can repel this sort
of danger. If we do not possess such logic and knowledge,

we must endeavor to attain it as our first priority. Islam furnishes us with such a capability. And if some Muslims are devoid of it, the fault lies with them, not with Islam.

If, God forbid, some people want to impose their rigid thinking on Islam and call it God's religion — since they lack the intellectual power to confront the opposite side's thinking on its own terms — they resort to fanaticism. This merely harms Islam, without achieving the aims of those people.

In rejecting the West we wish to free ourselves from its political, mental, cultural, and economic domination, for as Muslims we differ from them fundamentally in world view and values. Thus, to understand our points of contention and for negating the rival's domination, we have no choice but to appraise and understand the West precisely and objectively.

We have to keep in mind that Western civilization rests on the idea of "liberty" or "freedom." These are indeed the most cherished values for humanity in all ages, and to be fair, Western civilization's march from the Middle Ages to modern centuries has broken many superstitions and chains in thought, politics, and society. The West has indeed freed humans from the shackles of many oppressive traditions. It has successfully cast aside the deification of regressive thinking that had been imposed on the masses in the name of religion. It has also broken down subjugation to autocratic rule. These are all positive steps and adaptive to the traditions of creation. Yet, at the same time, the view of the West about humans and freedom has been rigid and one-dimensional, and this continues to take a heavy toll on humanity.

When confronting the opponent in the name of rejecting the West and defending religion, if we stifle freedom we will have caused a great catastrophe. Neither the traditions of creation allow this nor does Islam desire it. But if rejecting the West means critiquing its view of freedom, humanity, and the world, then we will have achieved our most fundamental historical mission.

Indeed, we take issue with the West on the notion of freedom. We do not think that the Western definition of freedom is complete. Nor can the Western view of freedom guarantee human happiness. The West is so self-absorbed in its historical setting and thoughts that it cannot see the calamities that its incorrect view of humanity and freedom has caused. If we look at the West from the outside, we can objectively judge this issue. But achieving this important task requires much intellectual rigor and knowledge.

Benefiting from the West's Experience

As Western civilization becomes increasingly worn out and senile, humanity is today searching for a new vision for its future, awaiting a new civilization which is more capable of meeting its material and spiritual needs and wants. Through our Islamic revolution, we have endeavored to create a new system whose values and visions differ markedly from what is prevalent in the Western-dominated world. Can we claim that our Islamic revolution has opened a new chapter in human history?

As noted above, no civilization is independent of the influences of those that have preceded it. The nature of the human mind does not allow it to suddenly and completely dispense with the experiences and knowledge of previous times. The secret of the evolution of human life on planet earth is that every person and generation starts its movement where others have left off. If all generations started and ended at the same point, human destiny would be no different from that of bees. The difference between humans and other social animals is that humans learn from their past experience, improve upon it, and leave their achievements for the next generation. And this process has continued uninterrupted for as long there has been a human race. Thus, there is no limit to human evolution.

Civilization, which is the fruit of humans' intellectual, emotional, and practical endeavors, works the same way. A vibrant, civilization-building thought is a thought that incorporates all the positive aspects of the previous civilizations, digests it, and adds to it.

Now, on the basis of our popular revolution we wish to construct an Islamic system. But we can only think of our revolution as giving rise to a new civilization if we have the ability to absorb the positive aspects of Western civilization and the wisdom to recognize the negative aspects of it and to refrain from absorbing them. This means that if we can break through the dead ends that the West has reached because of its values, and pass through them unscathed, we will succeed in our mission.

If we must adopt the positive features of Western civilization, simultaneously casting aside its deficiencies, we have no choice but to understand the West correctly and comprehensively in the first place. We must judge it fairly and objectively and learn from and use its strengths, staying clear of its defects by relying on our revolution's Islamic values. And it is obvious that this approach is different from a rigidly political appraisal of the West. Those who cannot separate the political West from the nonpolitical West are acting against the interests of the nation and the Islamic revolution, even though they may be doing so inadvertently. Here, introspection, rationality and objectivity will be effective, not harsh words and violence.

The Difficulties of Our Revolution

In all fairness, our Islamic revolution has been the source of great transformations in many corners of the world, and we, as the source of revolution, are naturally the most affected by these transformations. In the wake of our revolution we have a mission which is as grand and formidable as the challenges we encounter. Passing through this difficult stage requires much wisdom and farsightedness, as well as patience and perseverance.

Although Islam had existed for centuries in the collective consciousness of believers as a collection of thoughts and values, our revolution propelled it into the contemporary political and social sphere, where it stands steadfast against its opponents. At the same time, this development has brought three novel challenges to the fore: our people's expectations, the opponent's treachery and conspiracy, and discord within our society.

First, our people's expectations. Now that a new system based on new ideas has taken over the reins of governance, people expect a great deal from it. This is especially true of those who have sacrificed for the system. Before the Islamic revolution people did not have many expectations because our economy, culture, politics, and educational system were dominated by the enemy, giving us the sense that we were not masters of our own fate. But as an Islamic and independent government has come to power — as all of the state's resources have been placed in Islam's hands — people have the right to expect the fulfillment of their needs and wants.

People wish to know specifically how the new system will regulate their lives and guarantee their rights. They also want to know the system's policy toward science, and technology, as well as social justice and equity.

At this juncture people will not be satisfied with promises alone; they want real, tangible, and practical results. And our system will be successful only if it can meet these expectations.

Some expectations are undoubtedly unrealistic. No government can work miracles overnight and eradicate all bottlenecks. Nor have all of people's expectations been based on a realistic appraisal of available resources. It is conceivable that unrealistic visions as well as impractical and unattainable ideologies have spurred these exaggerated expectations. Still, government must have the power to satisfy people's needs and guide them to modify their expectations and views. If it is not possible to meet all expectations — and it is not — at least people have to be convinced that our orientation is generally toward a fulfilling life, focused on meeting their spiritual and material needs.

Our society has to believe that what the revolution has offered and what it expects of people will simultaneously meet individual and societal needs, utilizing all of society's human resources and achievements. Society must also believe that our system is not burdened with the shortcomings and strains that bedevil our opponents.

The natural expectations of people puts officials and the elite under great pressure to perform, and the enemy fans the flames of people's expectations in various ways.

Second, the opponent's treachery and conspiracy. Before the victory of our revolution we had many theoretical disagreements with opposing schools of thought. Those confrontations were easy to carry out because there was no real friction. But when ideas are put into practice and taken to the social and political sphere, opponents feel more threatened and thus resort to more violent and comprehensive confrontation.

Conspiracy to overthrow the revolutionary system, spying, economic pressure, fomenting pessimism and dejection among our people, attributing all our problems to the system's officials and portraying them as incompetent in meeting people's difficulties, and even resorting to military force for damaging the revolution and its popular base, are among actions taken by opponents who see their interests threatened by the new system. Our great nation in this period has experienced all sorts of enemy conspiracies. Just when the system and its managers need people's calm and optimism more than ever to focus all their thoughts and ingenuity on meeting society's needs, we encounter a heavy storm of enmity and conspiracy that sometimes forces us to focus our scarce resources on counteracting the danger posed by the foreign enemy and its domestic sympathizers.

These are among our greatest difficulties at this juncture. And there is no other way than to confront these realities. In the midst of these pressing difficulties, we must persevere and march on with patience, confidence, and wisdom.

Third, discord within. In the last hundred years our society has experienced two acute woes which have weakened and undermined its fabric. These woes have become more chronic and troubling at this sensitive juncture in our history. One is secular intellectualism, the other being unenlightened religious dogma.

The Secular Intellectual

Our society has a religious identity. All throughout Shiism's history the clergy have played a crucial role in awakening people to social pathologies, inciting them to fight injustice, awakening their religious identity. In our history, Islam has perpetually invited people to unity in religious belief, protecting their individual and social dignity. With their incessant calls to social justice throughout the history of Islam, populist religious leaders have served as society's most astute pathologists and healers.

That is why Muslim societies have never harbored a

negative view of religion. This stands in stark contrast to Western societies where unsavory and misguided religious leaders have turned people away from religion.

In the Muslim world, especially in Iran, whenever oppressed people have risen against tyranny, their activism has been channeled through religion. People have always witnessed the fiery and bloodied face of religious revolutionaries who have risen to fight oppression and despotism.

Our social conscience is replete with memories of the clash of true believers with hypocrites who have used religion to justify people's misery. Our part of the world has witnessed the historical antagonism between truth- and justice-seeking religion and the oppressive and misguided views of religion that have been the tool of oppressors.

Is it not true that in the history of Islam, religion has opposed religious and secular tyranny? Haven't most martyrs of truth been religious activists? Is it not the case that over the past hundred years religion has been the greatest champion of the fight against despotic agents of colonialism? Hasn't the experience of religious struggle, among other revolutionary and nationalist experiences — some of which are worthy of praise — been the most successful?

Our society is religious and it is natural that secular

intellectuals have never enjoyed a social base or a place in our people's hearts.

Unfortunately what has been called intellectualism in our society has been a movement that has been superficial and cut off from the people. Never has the voice of self-appointed intellectuals traveled beyond the cafeterias and coffee houses where they have posed as a political opposition. Even if people have heard their voice, they have found it incomprehensible. Thus, there has never been any mutual understanding.

And if public-minded intellectualism came to the fore and gained respect, it was through people who cast their claims in authentic, traditional, and religious terms. This was the reason for the vast popularity of figures such as Jalal Al-e Ahmad[3] and Ali Shariati.[4] These two were real intellectuals, and our society felt that they were a part of the people and spoke to the people's pains and concerns.

The secular intellectual, knowingly or not, pours water into the enemy's mill, the same enemy who is against our independence, who opposes our people's authentic culture, religion, and freedom. And history testifies that this group has on the whole been on the same side as, and has sometimes actively cooperated with, despotic systems propped up by foreigners. But fortunately, because it lacks deep roots in our culture and people's souls, it has not had much effect. And today also I believe secular intellectuals present no real danger, even though they may foment chaos in the minds of the young and other susceptible parts of society, or provide a foothold and opening for the enemy to penetrate society.

Religious Dogma

The other main problem we face is the parochialism and regressive visions of dogmatic believers. Religious dogma is nothing more than ascribing sanctity and eternity to limited and incomplete human interpretations, and giving priority to emotions over rationality and realistic appraisal.

If we ask dogmatic believers — who may see themselves as thinkers and intellectuals — what they expect from the revolution, they claim that they want a return to Islamic civilization.

We must alert such people that their wishes are anachronistic. The specific thoughts that underpinned Islamic civilization ended with the passing of that civilization. If it had maintained its dynamism, relevance and ability to provide answers to people's problems, that civilization would have endured.

Dogma presents the most formidable obstacle for institutionalizing a system that wishes to provide a model for the present and future of human life, a system based on a more powerful logic than competing schools and ideologies.

The effect of dogma on our society which has a religious identity is vast. And its negative effect is greater than secularism, especially because dogmatic believers usually project the aura of religious legitimacy. Their religious duties compel them to act but they have no connection to authentic Islam, the Islamic revolution, or to the present and the future.

Imam Khomeini,[5] especially in the last two years of his life, was deeply concerned with the danger that dogma and backward vision posed to the revolution's path and the progress and welfare of Islamic society. In line with all of Imam Khomeini's warnings, vigilance about this phenomenon is crucial to us and the future of the Islamic revolution.

The Void in Religious Intellectualism

Here I want to touch on one of the most important deficiencies of our society at this sensitive juncture, hoping that it spurs debate among thinkers, irrespective of whether they accept my proposition or reject or modify it.

In my view, the greatest defect we have in the sphere of thought and development is the lack or weakness of religious intellectualism, even though I see the ground as ripe for its emergence and growth.

An intellectual, in my view, is one who lives in his own time and understands the issues and problems confronting humanity in that period. He keenly pursues such knowledge, and because he understands the problems of the day, he represents the only hope for finding solutions to those problems. For how can we expect someone to solve a problem when he does not know that a problem exists? Here, moral rectitude will not suffice. Nor will knowledge by itself. A moral person who is a moving encyclopedia but lives outside his time, for whom the most pressing problems are for example the second and third Islamic centuries, cannot solve even the smallest of today's problems, for today's problems do not interest him.

In contrast, the main quality of an intellectual is that she lives in her own time, taking on a social responsibility, her mind constantly curious and restive about reality and human destiny. An intellectual is one who respects rationality and thinking and also knows the value of freedom.[6]

Who is a Religious Believer?

A believer is one whose vision of being transcends the small cage of the material, and while he sees humans as having come from nature, he does not see them as limited to the natural world. Instead he sees every human as bigger than the whole of nature, because nature is limited while humans are, in a way, limitless and eternal. Just as the questions and needs of humans know no limits, time and space cannot limit and circumscribe humans in their narrow bounds. And for this reason humans look at the future and at the past, and with the aid of their mental faculties break the bounds of nature to find the gateway to transcend it.

The religious intellectual is one who loves humanity, understands its problems, and feels a responsibility toward its destiny and respects human freedom. She feels that humans have a divine mission and wants freedom for them. Whatever blocks the path to human growth and evolution, she deems as being against freedom.

Our dynamic society at this sensitive juncture badly needs religious intellectuals. If religion and intellectualism are combined, we can hope that our great Islamic revolution will be the harbinger of a new era in human history. But if these two are separated, each will endanger the health of society.

When you mention God to secular intellectuals, they say they prefer to focus on humans. When you mention humans to the dogmatically religious, they say they prefer God. But the religious intellectual seeks "Godly humans," a creation whose emergence is as pressing a need today as it will always be.

I hope that through our revolution and a well-conceived connection between these two spheres — by connecting religious seminaries and the main centers of thinking in today's world, meaning universities — we will witness the emergence of the religious intellectual. This is a scenario that has neither the deficiencies of secular intellectualism nor those of dogmatic religious belief. Such a movement must shoulder the grand mission of our revolution and solve the crisis that is born out of the birth of a new system, all to benefit humanity, moving us toward a future replete with fulfillment and growth.

Notes

[1] This argument does not imply that each of the two types of crisis necessarily follows the other. Because of the connection of the "death crisis" of the first civilization to the "birth crisis" of the second, they must not be viewed as being identical because:

First, my focus is on the crisis that one civilization creates, one at the peak of civilization and the other at its nadir, not the crisis of the end of one and the birth of the second. Second, even if the crisis of the end of one civilization and the crisis of the birth of another civilization coincide, this does not mean that we should see them as the being one and the same, for these two crises are qualitatively different in nature, similar to the way life and death are different. Third, it is not as though as soon as a civilization dies there is immediately another one to replace it. Instead, a civilization comes, stays for centuries and then leaves. Different societies provide different breeding grounds for civilizations. To know this for certain requires greater and more careful scrutiny which this author has not had the chance to undertake. Nonetheless, we should not doubt the qualitative difference between these two kinds of crisis.

2The very quest for a "new world order" is an obvious sign that the current order is under serious strain as it fails to meet people's fundamental needs. The ever-more frequent and extensive discussion of the "new" order, especially in the West, is itself proof for the existence of a crisis in the West and in the rest of the world. We cannot overlook the fact that oppressive powers, led by the United States, continue their deceitful attempt to manipulate the current historical moment and world consciousness to assert their destructive domination of the developing world under the guise of the "new world order." This is an attempt to subvert and prevent fundamental transformations in the current order that would benefit all of humanity. There is voluminous material on the "new world order" which I defer to another occasion.

3Translator's Note: Jalal Al-e Ahmad (1923–1969). Seminal and prolific Iranian writer who popularized the effects of the cultural imperialism of the West or "Westoxication" among his generation.

4Translator's Note: Ali Shariati (1923–1977). Iranian sociologist and reformer of religious thought who played an important role in bridging the gap between Islamic thought and modern Iranian intellectuals. His numerous books and speeches, widely disseminated before the 1979 revolution, were instrumental in arousing Islamic revolutionary sentiment among Iranians.

5Translator's Note: Ayatollah Rouhollah Khomeini (1902?(1989). Leader of the Iranian revolution of 1979 and the founder of the Islamic Republic of Iran.

6My interpretation of the intellectual is based on convention. I use this concept to refer to actual, existing individuals. Others may have interpretations that do not allow a combination of intellectualism and religious belief. But it is unwarranted to confine ourselves to the prejudiced interpretation of a certain social group.

Religious Belief in Today's World

The question before us is the condition of religion in today's world, and the calling and difficulties the religious believer faces. We may refer to all religious believers, be they Muslim, Christian, or Jewish, but in the first instance I mean we Muslims, even though this may apply to non-Muslims who seek dignity and self-respect as well.

As a Muslim who wants to live in his own time, focused on a future in which he wants to be instrumental while remaining dignified, I put forward my question regarding religion. This is a personal question in that I do not speak as an impartial and neutral person, but as an interested Muslim who is inquisitive, even though it might be necessary in some instances to look at religion from the outside so that we are not mired in prejudice and we do not descend into the abyss of ethnocentricity. So when I ask what conditions we Muslims are in, both sets of questions, inside and outside views, must be clarified.

We Muslims once had a dominant civilization and were shaping human history in a way that we are no longer capable of today. We want to regain our place in history and, if possible, build a future that is different from our present and even our past, without rejecting those who are different from us, and without ignoring scientific thought and the practical achievement of humanity.

But what do I mean by "today's world?" Briefly, I mean "Western Civilization," which dominates the world. This means that our economic, political, social, and cultural life is strongly influenced by the West; without its legacy and achievements, life is impossible for us Muslims. We see the effect of the West everywhere: the design, and management of the city that we live in, communication technologies and much else that we use on a daily basis are all Western creations.

Today's world is Western in its orientation, techniques, and thoughts, such that even if one lives outside the geographic boundaries of the West, one must incorporate the West into one's values and life. The West has indeed brought great achievements to humanity, but it has also created great difficulties. But the key issue here is that our difficulties are more compounded than the West's because Westerners at least have a culture that is in harmony with their civilization and thus do not suffer from a precarious identity. But our problems are compounded precisely because on the one hand our personal and social lives are directly influenced by the West, a civilization whose foundations we have not absorbed and internalized. On the other hand, aspects of our culture belong to a civilization whose time has passed. Even though there is no definitive, ultimate view of what culture and civilization are, in my view civilization consists of the material aspects of social life and all institutions and organizations that act as political, economic, industrial, and other frameworks for social organization. Culture, the way I conceive it, is the collection of rooted beliefs, as well as habits of thought and emotion in society.

Some might see the West's crisis as being attributable to the antagonism between its motivations and human nature. We suffer from the same problem, albeit second hand. But the problem of non-Westerners is more acute because the culture that dominates our minds does not match the realities of life in this age. We suffer more severely from these contradictions than Westerners.

It is indeed possible to differentiate culture from civilization. A culture that is adapted to a civilization can remain in people's lives long after the demise of that civilization. Civilization is the basis and foundation of a culture; on the basis of its schism with culture, civilization loses its innovative and creative power, actually becoming an impediment in the way of development, for it is not deeply rooted and gradually comes apart.

One of our most central problems is that important aspects of our culture belong to a civilization whose time has long passed, and our life is influenced by modern civilization which requires a culture appropriate for it.

As Muslims who want to hold our heads high and maintain our historical identity, which for us is Islam, what are we to do?

Do not expect me to provide a manifesto on this, for I admit my own mental incapacity before such a grand task, and second, people's lives cannot be corrected by manifestoes. One of the most powerful manifestoes was that of Marx and Engels, and we saw what it led to, even though these two, especially Marx, were brilliant and powerful thinkers and the greatest pathologists of the capitalist order.

We must confess in all sincerity that life is a collective effort which cannot go forward except through debate, critique, and cooperation, and by recognizing the limitations and relativity of all perspectives. What we are proposing here is merely one set of possibilities, not a final and definite solution. We need more open debate and thoughtful and sincere participation in the process of serious questioning, and a more concerted effort in finding answers. First, let us look at religion.

Religion is among the oldest human institutions. Life in the absence of religious belief and resignation to a higher order is devoid of meaning. Whether they want it or not, humans have a sense of the infinite supernatural deep in their beings and grasp this from the depths of their souls. Humans are creatures that can understand the essence and secret of being and that is why they want to uncover the nature of being — witness how many secrets have been uncovered by human efforts so far. But existence is so complex that as soon as one question is answered, many more appear soon after. Humans knowingly live in a sea of mysteries and curiosity about being, dazzled by existence and all its complexity and intricacy. And religion is the most stable, firm, and sincere answer to people's awe before existence. I believe that until there is a human race there will be awe, and until there is awe the place of religion in the life and mind of humans is more secure than any other institution or phenomenon, for religion empowers the incomplete but curious human mind to grasp the all-knowing creator. There is no one who deep in his or her heart can deny the existence of the infinite and the transcendent. But people are affected by nihilism, ignorant of the transcendent reality — which is as harmful as the other extreme, which is thinking of transient and changing phenomena as eternal and static. Much of the catastrophes in history have originated from these two mistakes.

A Godless life, especially without the monotheistic

religions and the God of Muslim mysticism or *Erfan* —
which is different from the God of the superstitious or
even the God of philosophers — is dark and narrow.
This is a God that is at the peak of nobility and grandeur.
With all their limitations and inability, humans can
make direct contact with this God and establish a sincere
emotional and linguistic relationship with it. In an anx-
iety-ridden world replete with uncertainty, humans can
get in touch with the center of being and draw advice
and direction from this source. This is a God that is mag-
nificent and majestic. Humans are in love with it but
also reverent toward it. This relationship is different
from the weak's fear of the strong, similar to the anxiety
of the incomplete in search of fulfillment before a being
that is complete and free of needs. Reverence is the basis
of rectitude. True rectitude is all reverence, and reverence
is being free of the bounds of belonging to the earth. The
earthly are dependent on this world, but the truly reverent see the world as being at their disposal, merely a tool
for enriching the spiritual aspects of their being.

Of course, we have also had negative *Erfan* and piety.
These are all signs of the limitations and fallibility of
humans that must be explored. It is evident that the
believer who shuns the material world has more tranquillity and gratification than those who only possess
material comfort and wealth, for while the happiness of

the former is eternal, the latter — food and sexual desire — are transient, and because the means of their attainment are dependent on hundreds of factors, the anxiety of losing future pleasure kills the present pleasure.

Thus in all fairness religious belief is rooted in the depths of the human soul. And according to the *Holy Qur'an*, the human constitution is religious and monotheistic.

The essence of religion is holy and transcendent, and if we extricate these two qualities, we will not have religion anymore. And anywhere there is holiness and transcendence, there is also absoluteness. Here I want to touch on one of the biggest afflictions that threatens the religious life of people.

The human heart is in touch with the divine and the transcendent, and whenever the human conscience achieves union with this spirit, this is itself a signal that the essence of humanity is in touch with that transcendent reality which has been referred to as the spirit of God. But human existence has two facets: natural and Godly. Humans have their heads in the sky, but their feet on the ground, predestined to live on this planet. And because they live on this planet, their lives and minds are in constant flux, reflecting the dynamic nature of this world. Because they are natural beings, they are unsettled. Humans are circumscribed by time and space, and thus their thinking is relative and fallible, affected by history and hence dynamic. Neither the body nor the mind remain constant. Of course, I do not believe that all human perceptions are relative and that there are no constants in human life, but that most human constructs and all the guiding theoretical knowledge are indeed time-bound and temporary. Our knowledge is relative and constantly in flux. There is no escaping the relativity of our beliefs and knowledge, and humans have no choice but to carry on with this uncertainty and put their knowledge and skills to the test of trial and error and to modify them.

History is all about the evolution of beliefs and assumptions about the world. Has the human mind remained the same over history? All the diversity among different traditions, views, and religions, and even among the sects of the same religion is proof that no one can claim to understand all reality from all angles. For example, when we speak of Islam, which Islam do we mean? Abuzar's Islam, Avicenna's Islam, Qazali's Islam, Ibn Arabi's Islam, the poets' Islam, or the Sufis' Islam? These are all indisputable aspects of history attesting to the relativity of human understanding, even of religion. Today, irrespective of creed, we differ from our parents in thought and deed.

One of the main difficulties of the community of

believers is that on the one hand they take some realities to be absolute, transcendent, and holy, and on the other hand, since they are themselves relative, they see all this through the prism of the relativity of their own minds and bodies. And as long as they concede their limitations and the root of this contradiction, their internal problems will not create a catastrophe. The more acute malaise of believers appears when the absoluteness and holiness of religion affects the time- and space-bound and fallible human interpretations of religion, such that the prescriptions of a few may come to be viewed as religiosity itself. A believer is seen only as someone who subscribes to this specific view. Many frictions have their root here.

We have religion and a shared capacity for rationality that is the tool of communication and mutual understanding among humans, and if we believe, as many philosophers do, that the human mind is governed by some absolute concepts that are valid at all times and places, let us also concede that human understanding is so limited that these relative interpretations are fallible. And the wide spectrum of opinion and beliefs among different schools and within schools, is the most prominent proof for the veracity of this claim.

Does this mean that all doors to the absolute are closed to the human mind? We know that a number of

modern philosophers in the West have answered this
question in the affirmative. They have either denied the
existence of absolute reality or have at least proposed that
we have no way of comprehending these realities, and
thus many Western thinkers have reached the conclusion
that at least in this-worldly social life religion has to be
cast aside.

But for the pious who believe in the omnipotence of
God this can never be convincing, even though there is
no way of knowing this with certainty. To call ordinary
people to a place that they cannot reach would be
unwise.

In my opinion the only secure way of understanding
God is through the heart, not the mind, through direct
experiential contact, not the intellect. All religions have
emphasized this heavily. The leaders of Islam have taught
us that the intellect can be used to worship the compassionate God, not to understand it. In another place they
have suggested that the way to reach the absolute is worship, not extrapolating from the known to the unknown.
As said in the *Qur'an*, the way of the absolute and
enlightenment is worship and good conduct, and the
cleansing of the inside, meaning that the preferred way
to know God is direct experiential contact, not understanding. Of course, this in no way denies the importance of philosophical and scientific intellect, especially

in Islam which emphasizes their important role. But it is necessary to recognize the limitations of the intellect, and the true believer must travel the path of the heart. The truth of religious belief is an experience, not a thought, an experience based on self-development, controlling earthly desires, and resignation before the grandeur of existence, and enchantment by the loved one. If this path is traveled, humans will reach God. Understanding is an intellectual endeavor where through known concepts one can reach the unknown, and corresponding to the position of the person in space and time, the intellect is relative.

What I have said is not new, as is evident in many religious teachings. Great mystics have all warned about the inability of the intellect, saying that the reasoning mind is based on a wooden, unstable footing. The important point is that great philosophers such as Avicenna who had great faith in the deductive and inductive powers of the intellect, have never claimed that conceptual intellect can get us to God. The intellect, if it can go all the way, can only reach the vicinity of the transcendent, not to the divine itself.

The path of the heart is a path that leads us to truth and righteousness. The religious experience flows from the depths of the soul. Many philosophers and mystics have tried to pinpoint the intellectual underpinnings of the religious experience, but the path remains experiential, not intellectual.

The delicate point here is that the path of the heart, which is the sure way of getting to God, must be traveled alone; it cannot be achieved vicariously, nor can one transmit this sort of enlightenment to others.

At the same time humans are social beings who must live on the earth; such a being is in need of tools to share with others such that she can communicate with them. Language is an important agent of contact between humans, but language is an outward manifestation, a reflection of a psychological reality that exists in the human mind. Humans are capable of interpretation and transmitting their interpretations to others through language. One can understand through the intellect that the link between intellect and enlightenment is human understanding, and this understanding is often beyond the control of humans. Human talents know no limits, and truly, the grandeur of human existence cannot be limited to material and natural things, but humans are limited in time and place, and thus have truncated vision. Humans are affected by emotions, and their enlightenment must flow from this emotionality, but since this emotionality is relative and fallible, human interpretations cannot be absolute.

Humans have signs of the superior being in them,

but must use their fallible intellect that nature has bestowed on them to deal with nature. With this intellect humans try to make sense of two separate matters: the natural and the supernatural worlds. Despite the relativity of human understanding, some believers see the absoluteness of religion as being the same as their limited and incomplete view of religion. But with the passage of time and transformations in human life, old interpretations do not suffice anymore. Instead of shedding their truncated vision and looking at religious issues with open-mindedness to be able to develop a more complete and dynamic view of religion, they try to impose their disjointed thinking on reality. This is impossible in the long term and the source of much calamity in the short term.

Human views of nature today are vastly different from those interpretations in the past. Some have, of course, tried to give a holy veneer to human interpretations. In Christian history, a specific interpretation of the natural world was espoused by the Catholic Church and for centuries this static view did not allow new beams to be projected onto it, and what hardships this imposed on thinkers and scientists! But this thinking was slowly transformed and today very few people, be they Muslim, Christian, or of other religions, believe that the Holy books and direct contact with God can guide humans in understanding natural phenomena. Instead, all have accepted that to understand the world and nature we must use rationality and intellect to arrive at theories that are valid and capable of answering questions and fulfilling needs. These theories constantly await falsification, but this view is still not accepted in the human sciences. We must, of course, distinguish between theory and empirical observation, to allow for thinkers and philosophers who believe in some constant and general principles in the sciences.

All interpretations are limited, not only regarding knowledge of the natural world, but also religion. Yet the limited nature of the human understanding of religion will not undermine religion itself, unless believers mistake their interpretations of religion for religion itself. Much friction in history has arisen out of this mistake, making people suspicious of religion because specific interpretations change.

Serving religion in this age requires that we courageously distinguish between the essence of religion and the incomplete interpretations of humans such that religion maintains its central place deep in the hearts of believers, in a way that we can modify religious thinking to adapt to the demands of our time. Given the multiplicity of views of religion over history, we must ensure that we do not think that our view of religion is the only one. We must see to it that our reference to religious sources is guided by proper logic and clearly defined methods that are themselves in constant flux. True, these are sacred matters, but our interpretations of them are human. Only through this realization will humans open their minds to the experiences and innovations of others.

And it is only in this case that commensurable with questions and needs, which are constantly being renewed, we can achieve a more instrumental and useful understanding of religion. Of course, we cannot view all religious interpretations as being equally valid, just as we cannot view lay people's interpretations of the natural world as advanced physics or biology. Valid religious interpretation, similar to scientific thinking, requires that we be loyal to the authentic sources, which for Muslims are the *Holy Qur'an* and knowledge of past methods of reaching religious enlightenment. Still, all we are left with is our interpretations of religion, and the eternal life of religion is ensured by the realization that religiosity cannot be confined to any time- and space-bound interpretation. It is such a view that will open the door to the evolution of all facets of the believers' lives, without allowing misdirected thinking to inhibit thought and development, simultaneously upholding the essence of religion.

At the same time, a dynamic and instrumental view

of religion depends on being intelligently present in this world, capable of handling and shaping current realities without losing our historical identity. I my view, Western civilization is the powerful reality of our age, even though the West does not seem amicable to us politically, and few are the non-Westerners who have not seen the pain of the West's political and economic oppression either in the form of the old colonialism or the hegemonic policies of the West today. But the political-economic West is only one facet of that civilization. The whole of the West is a civilization that has its own culture, and this civilization is based on a specific world view and value system. Without understanding these values, our grasp of the West will be superficial and misleading. At the point of appraisal, we must shun the extremes of hating the West or being completely enchanted by it, so that on the one hand we can guard against the dangers posed by the West, and on the other hand utilize its human achievements. All this will be possible only if we reach a stage of intellectual and historical maturity to gain the capability to discern and choose, and accept the responsibilities inherent in this choice.

Fears and Hopes ❧

Even those opposed to our revolution's goals and ideals concede its greatness. Unprecedented conspiracies and planning against us offer ample proof that this revolution has been taken seriously, its greatness indisputable even to its enemies. The Islamic revolution has spread its momentum across the Muslim world and beyond. It has given new hope to Muslims and downtrodden peoples who seek freedom and justice, hence affecting the world's intellectual and political climate.

This sort of transformation cannot help but create friction and anxiety in the society that originated it. Thus, our society's post-revolutionary anxiety comes from the flux we are going through as we enter a new phase in our history. But this should be no cause for worry.

At the same time, proportional to its extent and seriousness, the fears and hopes that this transformation has given rise to are great as well: fear of all that threatens the revolution and hope for the bright, fulfilling future of revolutionary society.

Thus, we expect thinkers to know not only the pillars of the revolution but also the problems that it encounters. Thinkers must focus on the relationship of the revolution to current realities in the world. Only in this way can we preserve all that is true and just, changing what is not.

In my mind, the primary challenge confronting our revolution is the fundamental opposition or schism of its pillars to what is prevalent in today's world. The intellectual foundations and goals of our revolution are at odds with most globally dominant values, sometimes negating them altogether. This is only natural because every revolution opposes the current order, having arisen precisely for this purpose in the first place. But in our case, this opposition is particularly intense because of the power our opponent wields in the world of ideas.

The world opposed to our revolution possesses a mature, well-thought-out intellectual and political system that has been centuries in the making, fine-tuned by generations of seminal scientists and thinkers. A centuries-long tradition of invention and innovation has developed into a solid sociopolitical system whose main ammunition is the title it has to a deeply entrenched value system. Its political and philosophical vision commands a large, global audience and its system is backed by capable scientists and experts.

Our opponent also commands an awesome economic, political, and military power, more diverse and complex than anything we have seen in the past. But this should not intimidate us because great revolutions have come face to face with powerful intellectual and political systems in the past and succeeded in transforming them. We who claim that our revolution is great cannot be overwhelmed by the power of the revolution's opponents.

What makes our predicament more challenging, however, is that the West's intellectual, moral, and political system, as portrayed and propagated today, is attuned and adaptive to basic human nature. People are naturally drawn to it.

The champions of modern thought and civilization claim that their vision rests on "freedom," a claim that we must take seriously especially now that socialist thought has withered with the demise of Soviet communism. This has been taken to mean that a system based on Western notions of freedom is the only one that can endure.

The opponent of the Islamic revolution relies on the principle of "freedom" and derives much of its power from this because freedom represents a central, instinctive human goal. When freedom is depicted as allowing people to do whatever they desire, this depiction matches the strong human urge to live free of limitations. But in practice limitless freedom is not possible, and "freedom," the way the West defines it, is reducible to license or being free of the encroachment of others.

Thus, the yardstick here is the thought and will of humans, meaning that the majority must decide what the limits of liberty are and make laws and regulations on that basis.

Champions of modern values believe that no obstacles should be placed in the way of people that would prevent them from doing whatever they desire — unless these wishes conflict with the wishes of others. Although it must incorporate a series of human-designed restrictions, the system is in general agreeable with instinctive and basic human needs and desires which do not have to be learned. In other words, all of the physical, worldly inclinations that the current Western order satisfies are strong motivations in every human's life. No work or education is necessary to find these inclinations compelling, and a system that satisfies them seems highly attractive.

Our revolution, on the contrary, has called people to values whose attainment requires much will, effort, and labor. We base our system on abstinence, honesty, and rectitude, which are not inborn in human nature. And although humans have the talent to attain them, to achieve them they must labor over many difficulties and accept that paying moral dues requires much work.

Thus the opponent of our revolution, while possessing much economic, political, military, scientific, and technological power, puts forth a set of values that are agreeable with basic human needs and inclinations. This makes its system look as though it has a moral and utopian vision, too.

The West claims that it not only allows humans to be free of restrictions on their behavior and instinctive wishes, but that such a life is morally superior to all other systems because the main goal of human life — the will to freedom — is fulfilled.

True, humans are attracted to nothing the way they are attracted to freedom, and they have arguably never sacrificed as much for the attainment of any goal as they have for freedom. Today, humans are offered a system that invites them to eat and drink as they like, dress and speak as they wish, and to think freely. Simultaneously, the goal of life in such a system is prosperity and power, both viewed as serving the greatest, holiest goal of humanity, namely freedom. The West uses the most basic and hence powerful human instincts to solidify its position. This is misleading because despite what it claims, the West is far from achieving true freedom. We want a system based on abstinence and high morality that only comes through relentless endeavor and the courage to embark upon moral and spiritual growth. This is true freedom, but people need to be taught to see it this way.

What further fans the flames of antagonism between us and our opponent today is the power and reach of global electronic communications. In our era each person is effortlessly in contact with others in all corners of the world. The borders that separated societies in the past have vanished at the hands of new communication technologies that allow instantaneous transfer of information and news across continents. Our opponent also controls this vital resource, possessing the complex technical knowledge to mass-disseminate images and waves to the world community: an uncanny skill for public relations and manufacturing consent through sights and sounds using the most refined, complex, and effective methods of science and technology to win others over to its thoughts and lifestyle.

Ours is a time when no one can blind the individual mind to what goes on in the world. Everyone everywhere is defenselessly bombarded by a barrage of information on world events, guided by views that world powers want disseminated.

Our opponent does not tolerate societies that differ from it, seeking to nip all independent movements in the bud. The West thinks of nothing but its own interests, and if a people turn away from its values or refuse to serve its interests, it focuses all of its vast capabilities to force them to surrender or risk annihilation. And this is precisely why our revolution has encountered waves of conspiracies and pressures from the moment it was born.

We must clarify the relationship of our revolution to

the difficulties it meets abroad. But this should not make us ignore our own internal problems.

One of the most important difficulties we face is the separation of Islam from the practical demands of the social and political sphere. Now that our Islamic revolution wishes to institutionalize a new mode of individual and social life as we encounter the world and its realities, we suffer from a void in our ability to regulate society and human relations through Islamic ideas that work. For centuries Islamic thought has been artificially relegated to the sidelines. Islam has not been allowed to govern and regulate social relations. Instead, society's reins have either been in the hands of anti-Islamic forces or controlled by groups who have merely used Islam for self-aggrandizement, propagating it solely to legitimize their power and rule.

Real Islam, during this long hiatus, turned into a force of opposition against corrupt and obsolete systems which ruled in its name. Today, our revolution yearns to build a system based on real Islam. Still, even our vision of real Islam encounters inadequacies when it attempts to address today's practical problems.

We are fortunate that the relentless effort and struggle of courageous thinkers and clergy saved real Islam from falling prey to political vicissitudes by transferring knowledge of such an Islam to new generations, never letting it perish.

Islamic thought delves with unrivaled richness into matters that transcend time, space and material reality, shedding a profound light on issues above and beyond the workaday world. Islamic mysticism or *Erfan* is unique in the history of human thought. Compared to other systems of transcendental knowledge, *Erfan* is the best equipped to address supernatural phenomena. But today, as we wish to put Islam into practice and apply its teachings to the material social and political world, we encounter an intellectual void that can only be remedied if we rely on authentic Islamic sources, principles, and rules of conduct.

Our Islamic revolution's utopian visions were clearly articulated in the slogans that came to define our ideology in the early days of the revolution. These slogans either flowed directly from the minds of the people or were articulated by the aware, enlightened leadership and subsequently embraced by the masses.

Our goals may seem beyond reach at the moment. A value system is only as strong and durable as the realistic and practical affirmation of its tenets. It cannot exist in the realm of thought and imagination alone. To get to our ideal in an unideal world, we must achieve an appropriate balance among order, welfare, and pace in our society. If the rhythms of our society do not meet the demands of the times we live in, it is only natural that we encounter puzzles and difficulties. It is precisely here that we need a mental breakthrough. Arriving at a practical, workable system attuned also to the demands of the revolution must be given the highest priority.

Our society's fabric is strained by vice; economic and political difficulties loom large, and we still suffer from the diluted identity of Westoxication — neither ourselves, nor Western. But if the root of the problem is to be found elsewhere, and we can solve the problem at its root, we will succeed in overcoming other difficulties more quickly, with greater confidence and effect.

In practical matters, as we have depended on theology to give order to the individual and social world, we face serious inadequacies. This can mean only that our theology must evolve to meet the demands of the revolution and also the practical needs we have today. Here we can turn to the grand leader of the revolution, Imam Khomeini, who was a visionary Muslim leader, philosopher, theologian, and mystic. We turn to him to uncover the void and inadequacies we must overcome to achieve our goals:

> We must bring about the realization of the practical laws of Islam, undeterred by the deceitful West, the invasive East and their globally dominant modes of diplomacy. For as long as theology is trapped in the books and in the clergy's chests, there is no harm done to world devourers. And until the clergy are active in every sphere, they will not realize that reli-

gious authority and knowledge is not enough. Centers of religious education and the clergy must be abreast of the times and have the pulse of the present in their hands and know the needs of the future. Always a few step ahead of events, they must come up with effective responses. Our current methods of running our society are likely to change in the years ahead. And human society may come to utilize the issues facing Islam.

Khomeini, Rouhollah (Imam),
Sahifey-e Noor (The Book of Light).
Volume 21, page 100.

We all agree that the Imam soared at the peak of religious-mystical awareness. The yearning of the revolution for truth and justice blossomed under his leadership. Based on the Imam's thinking, a cleric who is unaware of the demands of his time, and lives with ideas that are hundreds of years old, will not be able to relieve society from today's strains, however noble his intentions might be. As well as understanding today's demands he must have the pulse, thoughts, and needs of the future in his hands, so he can shape events instead of being at their mercy. The Imam says in another place:

In Islamic government there should always be room for revision. Our revolutionary system demands that various, even opposing, viewpoints be allowed to surface. No one has the right to restrict this. It is crucial to understand the demands of society and governance such that Islamic government can make policies that benefit Muslims. Unity in method and practice is essential. It is here that traditional religious leadership prevalent in our seminaries will not suffice.

Ibid, page 47.

And,

One of the greatest problems of religious leadership is the role of time and place in decision making. Government specifies a practical philosophy for dealing with sacrilege and internal and external difficulties. But these problems can not only not be solved by a purely theoretical view of religion but will lead us to dead ends and the appearance that constitutional laws have been breached. While you must ensure that religious infractions do not happen — and I hope God doesn't bring that day — you must focus all your effort on ensuring that when encountering military, social and political issues, Islam does not seem to lack practical utility.

Ibid, page 61.

And on another occasion,

But on the question of the educational methods and research in religious schools, I believe in traditional theology and deem straying from it to be inappropriate. Religious leadership is proper and correct only in this way. But this does not mean that Islamic theology is not dynamic. Time and place are two determining elements.

Ibid, page 98.

We should not doubt that many of the views that have guided us thus far are not sufficient for managing social affairs. We must achieve a new vision and understanding. Relying on current religious leadership is necessary but not sufficient.

If this central concern is overshadowed by peripheral matters, society will be held back from achieving a desirable solution to problems. Serious as these problems are, however, we cannot lose our hope in the future. Most important, our young intellectuals must maintain an active and hopeful presence on the social stage.

The late Imam was an irreplaceable blessing for our revolution and the establishment of the Islamic Republic. His legacy remains a great reviver of God's religion in our time. His main difference from other religious revivers is the central leadership role he played in the establishment of Islamic government. He was aware that if religious leaders, thinkers, and intellectuals are not confronted with practical problems, they will not think of solutions. But when Islam came to the political scene, established a government, and took power into its own hands, it confronted the necessity of fulfilling the rational expectations of all people who had put their hopes in the revolution. This encounter was a great step toward the establishment of a new system of thoughts, values, and skills appropriate for our time and place, capable of addressing human needs within an Islamic framework.

The Imam's greatest legacy is indeed the establishment of Islamic government, which has managed to stand despite many pressures and conspiracies against it. The enemies may have hoped that after the Imam's passing away, the system's pillars would unravel. But with the grace of God this did not happen. The institutionalization of leadership after the Imam and our continuing in his path of revolutionary struggle are a source of great hope to us all.

Another source of hope is the current condition of humankind in our era. Our Islamic revolution has raised a storm across the Islamic world and among all of the world's downtrodden. Thus the utopian yearnings and explosive power latent in the hearts of the world's dispossessed greatly buttress our revolution. If we understand this force and use it effectively, we will be able to confront the opponent despite its economic, military, and political predominance. If we rely on the utopian visions that our revolution has awakened throughout the Islamic world and beyond, and believe that backers of our revolution are ready to sacrifice for it, victory is within our reach.

What adds further hope to our future is that our opponent — despite all its apparent might — has gotten old and is approaching the end of its line. The existence of crisis in the thought and civilization of the West betrays its senility.

Again, our main problem is the fundamental opposition of the values of our revolution to what is dominant in the world on the one hand, and our lack of practical experience in installing a real religious government on the other. What must we do to solve this problem so that with the help of God we can ensure that this revolution remains immune to serious threats?

The unsophisticated among us may opt for the simplistic option of censorship and preventing the values and thoughts of our opponent from reaching and subverting our people. But is this a viable solution?

The low capacity and truncated vision of some may lead them to attack all that does not fit into their closed minds and match their tastes as being against Islam, the revolution, and the legacy of the revolution's martyrs. Unfortunately, there are camps in our society, which although bereft of proper logic, think of themselves as the pillars of the revolution and Islam, and accuse their opponents of being against Islam and the revolution, as they try to oust their opponents from the political ring at any cost.

But what exactly is the yardstick for judging what is acceptable and what is not? In opposing difficulties and the enemy, what strategy should we adopt? Will our cultural policy be one of censorship and restricting access to all sources we disagree with? Can a policy of isolation from the international community succeed in today's world?

Throughout its glorious history, Islam has never accepted isolation and restricting access as a viable policy. In certain periods this has been imposed on people in the name of Islam, causing irreparable damage, but it has not lasted. Islam has embraced opposing views with open arms. Seminal Muslim thinkers have actively sought the encounter of other views. This openness has imbued Islamic civilization with much intellectual weight.

At the same time restriction is not practical in today's world. Information channels accessible to our people are not limited to government-run sources. Let us assume that we prevent all faulty prose from being published, stop all newspapers or magazines from printing the smallest bit that offends our tastes, or disallow the production of any films that we find defective. Will these thoughts and views that have been officially banned find no other channel of reaching our people?

In judging what is good and bad in the world of ideas, rigid fixations and dogma may replace strong logic and realistic appraisals much to our detriment. It is naïve to think that government-run channels are people's only source of access to international and inter-societal communication.

Today, the global broadcast of mass-communicated

electronic images and vibes is under no government's control. How can we prevent dynamic and curious minds from accessing what they desire? How can we build a wall between such minds and the outside world? With the rapid advance of communication technology that is becoming accessible to ever-larger segments of our population, controlling the spread of images will only be more unrealistic and impractical in the future.

Of course this does not mean that our Islamic system should impose no limitations and restrictions on people's access to information. That would be unrealistic as well. No form of governance can exist without imposing some restrictions, and even the most developed liberal democracies are not exempt from this rule. But there is a difference between a system that relies on restriction as its main strategy and a system that uses restriction occasionally to deal tactically with sensitive and vital matters. Any system is bound to impose some form of restriction when its whole existence and the fundamentals of its rule are endangered. However, on the whole Islam historically has not based its system on restriction and censorship.

The cultural strategy of a dynamic and vibrant Islamic society cannot be isolation. As a progressive religion Islam shuns building fences around people's consciousness. Instead, our strategy must focus on making our people immune, raising and educating them to resist the cultural onslaught of the West on their own. Only a strategy of immunization represents a viable solution for today and tomorrow. This requires us to allow various disparate views to engage one another in our society. How is it possible to make the body immune without injecting it with a controlled and weakened virus, so that it can resist the more extensive and threatening invasion of that virus? The way to make the body resistant to viruses is certainly not by preventing any viruses from coming near it. Instead we must see to it that the living organism has the apparatus to resist the virus itself. In society, too, it cannot be any other way. An active, evolving society must be in contact and communication with different, sometimes opposing, views to be able to equip itself with a more powerful, attractive, and effective thought than that of the opponent. And if the sources of revolutionary and religious thought really wish to preserve the revolutionary system, they have no other choice than to offer society sophisticated and adaptive thinking.

At the outset of the revolution, the Imam (Khomeini) counseled against shutting out what we found undesirable. And we are proud that our revolution took its first steps on the basis of liberty. This was not an unintended consequence of the revolution, out of our leaders' hands. The principle from the beginning was that others can speak their minds, unless they are engaging in conspiracy. If there were groups who did not want to use this freedom wisely and fairly, abusing and subverting it instead, they were the ones at fault, not the revolution. Society suffered great harm as a result of their unseemly actions. It was the abusers of liberty who did not uphold the supremacy of thought and rationality as they tried to pollute the atmosphere of openness and use it for imposing their autocratic wishes. They did not realize that a government held up by the will and belief of a people and watered by the blood of martyrs and the effort of millions of selfless devotees will stand firm against conspiracy. The limit of legal opposition was conspiracy then and it must be the same today.

The idea of what exactly constitutes conspiracy must be clarified as well. We must look at social problems with a comprehensive and open view. Otherwise any closed-minded and dogmatic person can use the excuse of conspiracy to oust her opponents from the political stage. Our system needs accountability and discipline.

Reckless and superficial but politically charged ideas of certain groups can neither determine society's best interests nor understand conspiracy and its limits. Otherwise, anyone can mount an attack on thoughts different from his own limited tastes with the excuse of defending the interests of the country, the revolution, and religion against conspiracy.

Thus, to solve our fundamental problems, we should build and offer superior thinking and logic, as well as more attractive solutions to society's woes. Only in this way can we give hope to the revolution's devotees, adding to their material and spiritual well being. We must endeavor to build a system so solidly grounded that it can not only resist unraveling at the encounter of other systems but can display its vigor and superiority. This impetus to self-affirmation has protected and enriched Islamic thought and the essence of religious belief over the ages.

A system like ours, based as it is on Islamic utopian ideology, is bound to restrict some individual liberties. A revolutionary religious system will naturally forbid much that is accessible to people — particularly the youth — in the West. The overflowing urges of the youth are better satisfied in the West, and hedonistic instincts are fulfilled to a greater degree; whereas in an Islamic system, a multitude of religious rules stand in the way. To make our society stable and strong we must teach the young a more worthy path than hedonism, such that they gain pleasure out of abstinence.

Utopian visions can keep people, especially the youth, confident and lively. Muslim youths must believe that alongside the limitations and restrictions that our system has imposed, it has given them character, imbuing their lives with a direction in whose shadow they feel pride, greatness and tranquillity. Emotional and mental needs must be addressed for people to feel content. If the Islam we offer fails to accomplish this, the foundations of our society will be unstable.

Fulfilling the utopian vision of the revolution's devotees inside and outside Iran is a pressing necessity to ensure our survival. To assert our identity it is necessary to be present in all world forums and to defend Islam and Iran effectively in all international tribunals and conventions. But we cannot ultimately flourish and make our weight felt in the international scene — whose rules are set by our opponents — unless we maintain our unique idealism. Why was it that we had less pressing cultural problems during the eight-year war with Iraq? Because a massive wave of revolutionary youths was at the front lines and people saw themselves as defenders of the revolution and the country. This active presence filled people with deep pride. Our youth felt that their lives had assumed new meaning, and that they had achieved spiritual growth with which they could stand against oppressors and tyrants. Now that the war is over, what must replace it? The only effective solution is preparing the ground for the active involvement of the young generation in all areas where their talents can develop and be put to productive use. If the young generation does not feel active and instrumental in society, it is natural that they feel dejected.

To make society vigorous, thinkers must see in Islam a system of superior logic and ingenious solutions. At the same time, all social forces must be active in the social and political process. Here the greatest mission of intellectuals is to understand the real Islam, the kind that our revolution drew from to succeed.

We live in a world that in many ways is at odds with our Islamic revolution's orientation, and we want to organize our lives on the basis of Islam. It is necessary to find out exactly what sort of Islam we want to base our lives on. Here it is incumbent upon our seminaries and universities to answer this question. It is not as though there is no divergence of opinion on what Islam is. Over the past century, if not all of Islamic history, we have confronted three separate Islams. To decide what sort of Islam we want, we must stay clear of factional squabbles such that we can chart our future path on the basis of the right sort of Islam.

Traditionally, we have encountered a regressive, a diluted, and a real Islam. Which of these three was our revolution based on, and which one can save our society and bring honor and pride to it? We believe that the basis of our revolution is the real Islam, the same Islam that has roots in revelation and solid monotheistic perspectives — an Islam that believes in the inherent dignity of humans and wants enlightened happiness for humanity, a constantly evolving Islam that can find solutions to new puzzles as they emerge. All throughout history, this interpretation of Islam has defended against sacrilege and corruption, but it has never been given the opportunity to assert itself in the sociopolitical sphere.

It is imprudent to assume that since our revolution has succeeded and an Islamic Republic established, the victory of real Islam will be assured automatically. No, we face serious difficulties and dangers. But in the first instance, the devotees of real Islam must equip themselves with rationality, thought, and logic more than ever before. The battle of ideas is far more fateful and determining than political and military conflict. First, we have to see which Islam we have accepted and why. Only then will we muster sufficient moral and intellectual weight to confront our opponents. The experience of our revolution has taught us invaluable lessons that we cannot forget.

From the first days that the Imam (Khomeini) took center stage, he began his religiously inspired struggle against tyranny, dependency, corruption, cultural degradation, and American imperialism. Within the ranks of the educated and senior clergy, there were those who opposed the Imam's method of struggle and his interpretation of Islam. Some were sympathizers of the monarchy; others were driven by profit-seeking and self-serving motives. Most such people were not traitors but had an interpretation of Islam that did not suit the revolution. There were others who supported the Imam in the initial steps but backed away from supporting him when matters got more serious.

Many of those devoted to the Imam had endured imprisonment and exile to see the revolution through. These were and are good, dedicated people, but subsequently, when the time came to institutionalize the revolution, their view of Islam strayed from the Imam's.

In many cases after the revolution, when the issue of social justice and combating inequality was voiced, some screamed that Islam was in danger. I not am saying that all those who used the slogans of social justice and fighting inequality were on the right path. The issue here is the principle of social justice itself and that there were those who did not even want to bring it up, resisting all practical steps that we wanted to take to ameliorate the problem. Such people could not tolerate the fact that the Imam's Islam wanted social justice, and thus subverted all efforts in this direction. The Imam was compelled to confront this thinking bluntly, stating that on the basis of the Islam he had introduced, achieving social justice was among the primary goals of the revolution.

And there were those who felt that the place of women was the home, arguing that the presence of women in the workplace leads to corruption and moral decay. They were against higher education for women, and opposed women's involvement in social affairs. This was another view that was introduced under the guise of Islam. At the end of the first elected Majles (Parliament) after the revolution, a few influential circles tried to convince the Imam that women should not be allowed to run for seats in the Majles. The Imam confronted this thinking resolutely and defended women's right to take part in the elections. Or there were those who claimed that no one other than the clergy should be allowed to take part in politics. They were especially suspicious of university students and academics, labeling them "deviant" just because they carried intellectual weight. They forbade a large part of society from being involved in the their own political destiny. They would try to justify all this in the name of Islam. Once again, the Imam responded swiftly, scolding their regressive prescriptions.

Some criticized all social and cultural programs to the point of forcing the Imam to outline explicitly the benefits of cultural activities to dispel any doubts. Others were opposed to all music, film, and theater. They were not against only some forms of art, but all artistic expression in general. Some even opposed broadcasting sporting events on television and thought it sinful. The Imam confronted all these restrictive and regressive religious views head-on, claiming that much of what they objected to was actually beneficial to society. In the last years of his prolific life, the Imam put forth the most penetrating critique of religious dogma:

> We must endeavor to break the chains of ignorance and superstition to reach the prophet's fresh fountain. Today the most puzzling thing to people is this Islam, and its rescue requires sacrifice; pray that I am myself one of these sacrifices.
>
> *Ibid, page 41.*

All who truly believe in the revolution and wish to dignify Islam will choose the Islam articulated by the Imam. This should not be taken to mean that others do not have the right to publicly express their views. Everyone is entitled to voice his opinion within the law and the bounds of rationality. However, we must know which interpretation of Islam our revolution is based on. Do the groups that our Imam numerously scolded have the right to impose their extreme views on the people and to portray their opponents as being against Islam and the revolution?

Regressive and dogmatic clerics, those whom the Imam singled out as the greatest danger to the revolution, are not sitting idly by. The enlightened and truly devoted must be mindful of the danger they pose and guard against it.

Alongside the regressive version of Islam, we have the camp that believes in a diluted Islam, a fabricated, inauthentic form of the faith that merely goes through the motions of piety without any real knowledge of Islam or real belief in its teachings. Their Islam has so many foreign, imported elements that it cannot be called Islam at all. Diluted Islam represents one of the most dangerous pores for the West's cultural onslaught. Un-Islamic or anti-Islamic political currents have never enjoyed a popular base and they have never been viewed as the main danger. But those who have had the appearance of piety and have been active in society with ideas borrowed from the West or others have been able to propagate their views in parts of society.

Opposed to these regressive and diluted views of Islam, we must recognize the real Islam, and the secret of our survival and success is the understanding and implementation of this kind of Islam, in whose shadow we can pass safely through dangers that threaten the existence and health of the revolution and our society. This is the same Islam that the late Imam epitomized, and for which a great mind like Motahhari[1] was martyred. We must discover the target of the Imam's pronouncements, particularly in the last years of his life. A bit of focus will show that the Imam's criticism was directed at those views of Islam that hinder progress and development, paralyzing the search for solutions to difficulties that face our society.

If diluted Islam martyred Motahhari, then regressive Islam has tried to negate the substance of his thought. The confrontations that have been directed at the likes of Motahhari and Beheshti[2] in our society are alarming and serious. And we even witnessed how unseemly this current was to Hashemi-Rafsanjani[3] when he brought up the issue of social justice. To know the real Islam and to base our society upon it, our greatest source of inspiration is the religious and devoted youth in our seminaries and universities. Aided by the knowledge and piety of eminent clergy, we must breed a new cadre of religious intellectuals who are up-to-date and enlightened, and we must tirelessly march toward understanding the specific vision of Islam that is the basis of our revolution. It is understanding and explaining this Islam that will make us immune to other schools of thought.

Notes

[1] Translator's note. Morteza Motahhari (1919–1979). Iranian thinker and cleric who was instrumental in reconciling traditional seminaries with universities. His writings made traditional Islamic concepts and the relationship between Iran and Islam accessible to his contemporaries. He was assassinated by armed opponents of the Islamic Republic a few months after the revolution.

[2] Translator's note. Mohammad Hosseini-Beheshti (1921ñ1980). A cleric and leading ideologue of Iran's Islamic revolution who was assassinated along with scores of other political figures when a bomb exploded in the headquarters of the Islamic Republican Party.

[3] Translator's note. Ali-Akbar Hashemi-Rafsanjani (b.1933). A cleric and

political leader in the Islamic Republic of Iran who has served in a number of senior posts culminating in his tenure as President of the Islamic Republic of Iran from 1989 to 1997. In 1997, he was appointed as chairman of the Expediency Council, a high-ranking consultative body.

Observations on the Information World ⁓

Much has been said in our era about the central role of information in shaping human destiny, making it possible even to claim that information has surpassed military and political might as the main source of power in today's world. All peoples who seek pride, power and progress must learn to manage this vital resource, staying abreast of constantly evolving communication technologies.

Timely access to information and effective means of disseminating it are central to the development process in every country. We cannot afford to fall farther behind in this rapidly advancing field and must cooperate to produce, store and disseminate information effectively. This is no easy feat.

Most inquiry into the information world focuses exclusively on its technical underpinnings at the expense of exploring its human, political dimension. This task is crucial to our destiny.

In its contemporary, complex forms, information

technology represents one of the highest achievements of modern culture which uses its control over information to solidify its domination of the world. Thus, inquiry into the nature of the information world is inseparable from uncovering the nature of modern civilization itself. And until we address this important question we will not be able to muster the confidence and wisdom to understand our relationship to modern civilization. Otherwise, we will live in a world whose rules have been set by others, at the mercy of circumstance, not as masters of our fate.

We confront the Western-dominated information world on two fronts: the realm of scientific information, and the realm of information that has sociopolitical and cultural significance. In the first case, the scientific method is unanimously regarded as the most authoritative way of understanding the world.

Science has spurred great transformations in human life, and no nation or people can survive without its blessings. Scientific underdevelopment and falling behind the era's technological breakthroughs have a pitiful effect. Yet the globally preeminent importance of science should not prevent us from asking fundamental questions about the human context of the scientific and technological enterprise. We cannot deify and worship science as though it were beyond the purview of human judgments.

Inquiring into the nature of modern science is especially necessary for us Muslims who once had seminal, world-class scientists but have now fallen behind the West in this sphere. We have been relegated to being passive consumers of the West's modern civilization. But if we use our rationality and wisdom, we will have the opportunity to break out of our current second-rate status, and we will be able to affect the course of human destiny.

In the eighteenth century, Westerners embraced the magic of science and technology. Grand theorists such as Kant designed their metaphysical systems to match the tenets of the physical sciences. Yet despite the optimism of eighteenth-century Europeans, people have come to realize that science is incapable of solving a broad range of problems that fall outside its purview.

Today, even the most loyal advocates of modern culture — and the socioeconomic and political system that it has given rise to — think of science as a series of tentative conjectures that constantly await falsification by newer and more complete theories. No one has the last word in the realm of science, for science is nothing more than what scientists perceive and perform. There is no way of knowing for certain that the subjective judgments of scientists accurately depict reality. Today, the objectivity of science has been brought into question more than ever before.

It is true that science has demonstrated remarkable effectiveness in solving practical puzzles, and there is no choice but to use its techniques of trial and error. Still, despite the optimism of eighteenth-century Europeans, we cannot base the whole social order on the institution of modern science which is impotent in addressing the metaphysical, philosophical, and mystical yearnings of humans.

Of course, our concerns with the limitations of science do not imply that we must return to the Middle Ages. Nor can we regress to the limited and backward views of religion and spirituality prevalent in those times. Modern humans need new interpretations of spirituality and supernatural phenomena to imbue their lives with meaning. Because of the central place of science and technology in Western civilization, uncertainty about their meaning has led to a general crisis in the West.

This crisis is more acutely felt in the human sciences than in the physical or natural sciences. Modern civilization is more deeply tied to political, cultural, and economic ideas than to the natural sciences. In the human sciences the subject and object of study are the same as humans study themselves, their societies, and their political systems. Inquiry is based on the motives and assumptions of the agent or the scientist, not on objective reality. And the identity crisis of the scientific community naturally will permeate the cultural and political sphere.

The flood of information in our age saturates the senses of all humanity so extensively that the ability to assess and choose is impaired even among Westerners who are producers of information, let alone us who have played a peripheral role in the information world. Electronic information is the brainchild of modern civilization. Thus the power of today's information-based mass culture is tied to the legitimacy of the values of Western civilization for which the information revolution counts as the most prominent achievement.

For those of us outside the West, the information world poses manifold challenges. Today, information is used by advanced industrial countries as the main tool of safeguarding their own economic and political interests, even if they are irreconcilable with the interests of the majority of the world's peoples who live outside the sphere of modern civilization.

Thus, however optimistic some might feel about the benefits of the information revolution for all humanity, we cannot doubt that politically and culturally loaded information is manufactured to protect the interests of industrialized powers while appropriating the rights of deprived and subjugated peoples. As consumers of such information we cannot ignore that the political will behind information production and dissemination is based on maintaining Western supremacy. Non-Westerners are taught to respect Western supremacy as legitimate, even desirable. Western civilization has used and continues to use all its resources to dominate the minds and lives of all peoples through controlling the sources of information and the means of communication.

This does not mean that we must isolate ourselves from the Western-dominated information world. Such a thing is undesirable and practically impossible as the global reach of information constantly expands. Awareness of today's world events is an imperative for understanding our place in the world and planning our future in it. Being isolated from the world's information networks can only turn us into pawns of others because it is they who control the flow of this vital and strategic resource.

We must reach a level of historical evolution and social maturity to be able to judge accurately the thoughts and efforts of others so that we know our place in the world and can put our own house in order. This way we can choose what benefits us in the new world and reject all that does not. We must become active on three fronts.

First, we must understand the peculiarities of our era and treat Western civilization as our era's ultimate manifestation and symbol. This means understanding the values and tenets of Western civilization and freeing ourselves from the equally harmful extremes of either hating it or being completely taken in and entranced by it. Second, we must try to come to grips with our own historical identity which has brought many valuable gifts to humanity but has also encountered many difficulties and inadequacies. And third, while we must pay attention to problems that threaten our society from the outside — the hegemonic nature of Western politics, economics, and culture — we must also focus on our own internal problems and frictions.

Many of our traditions are human constructs that, however great they might have been in their own time, belong to a different historical epoch and place but have nonetheless maintained the veneer of sanctity and infallibility. Today, dogmatic attachment to archaic ideas poses a serious obstacle to our society, preventing it from utilizing the human achievements and thoughts of our era. Let us not forget that not just the natural world, but religion must also be scrutinized by reflection, for our interpretation of religion is constantly being modified as well.

Our attachment to the past should not mean negating all the achievements of modern, Western civilization. We will not return to the past to stay there, but merely to understand and regain our identity that has been rendered fragile by the onslaught of Western culture. With knowledge and will, we can shape the future, which beckons the cooperation and coordination of all devotees and thinkers of the Muslim world. We Muslims have a grand historical legacy that we must revive in today's world.

Despite disagreements among sects within the Islamic world, the unity and coordination of Islamic thought across various parts of the Islamic world has been phenomenal. Over centuries of Islamic history, Andalusian theologians preached in Damascus and Baghdad, just as Persian philosophers and mathematicians felt at home in Africa and Mesopotamia. We Muslims possess the foundations for a solid unity that can create a powerful cultural movement in the future.

First, we possess a common historical bond and system of values that Islam, as the source of a great civilization, has provided us. Although this civilization is no longer globally dominant as it once was, it represents the greatest source of shared experience among all Muslims. Our attachment to the theism of Islam, based on a belief in the unity of God, is the linchpin of the bond that ties all Muslims together.

Second, the increasing awareness of all peoples, especially in this century, has instilled a sense of unity of purpose among Muslims as we all perceive ourselves as the victims of colonialism in its various forms. There is no one among us who has not seen his dignity, freedom, and independence violated by colonial powers. We all wish independence and freedom from the shackles of this domination. If we combine our common pains and unify our visions and beliefs, we will sow the seeds of betterment and prosperity in our societies. Sharing and coordinating our information resources represents the hallmark of this cooperation.

The Islamic Republic of Iran, despite its many differences with the globally dominant political order, has always championed deep cultural and scientific ties among Muslims of all countries. And today also, we believe that despite political differences the conditions must be created for the scientists and thinkers of the whole Muslim world to work together. All Muslims must firmly join hands to further the cause of development in their societies.

Covenant with the Nation

Presidential Inaugural Speech

at the

Islamic Consultative Assembly (Majles)

August 4, 1997

In the name of God,
the Compassionate, the Merciful

With the grace and benevolence of God Almighty, and relying upon His omnipotence, here in the House of the Nation, and in the presence of the honorable heads of the Legislature and the Judiciary, members of the Council of Guardians, members of the Assembly of Experts, representatives of the Islamic Consultative Assembly, respected scholars, thinkers, and government officials, distinguished Iranian and foreign guests and in front of all my noble Iranian sisters and brothers, I would like to bring to your august attention a number of observations with respect to the heavy responsibility being entrusted, as of today, to this humble servant.

Fulfillment of the obligation to serve the Islamic Republic, the concrete embodiment of a popular revolution, is indeed a great honor. Endeavors towards safeguarding this system and further advancing its stature and authority, as well as the betterment of the spiritual and material life of the courageous people of Iran, constitute an important responsibility for all those committed to Islam, the Revolution, and Iran.

The noble people of Iran, through their great, conscientious, and discerning presence and participation in the seventh presidential elections, created an epic of historical proportions, thus exhibiting their trust and confidence in their cherished system of governance. Now, the popularly elected Executive branch, along with the other two·branches of government, carries heavy responsibilities in response to such a popular and national trust and expectation. The framework and the outline for this heavy responsibility is defined in the Constitution. The Constitution, the covenant of our Islamic and national solidarity, the actual embodiment of popular allegiance to the Islamic Revolution and the great ideals of the late Imam Khomeini, and the document paid for with the blood of our noble martyrs including [President] Rajaie and [Premier] Bahonar, serves as the fundamental reference for the powers and responsibilities of the government and the rights and duties of citizens. Therefore, to serve the people, it is incumbent upon the Executive, and is likewise the mandate and mission of the President of the

Islamic Republic, to endeavor towards institutionalizing the rule of law, and the Constitution, first and foremost.

This is the only way the continuity of the Revolution, the dynamism of the system, and the power and dignity of the noble people of Iran can be ensured. Hence, our honorable people, led by His Eminence Ayatollah Khamenei, can witness the establishment and preservation of the institutions emanating from the Revolution within the framework of a strong and vibrant society and a stable and law-based structure.

At this juncture, at the beginning of a new phase in the administration of the country and in pursuance of the valuable and admirable efforts of Hojjatol-Eslam Hashemi-Rafsanjani — whose legacy of deeds, ideas, and experience will continue to be a great asset for us all — the new government, hoping to draw upon the precious accomplishments of previous administrations during the periods of sacred defense and reconstruction, assumes great responsibilities.

Within the framework of such a responsibility, and before the Holy Qur'an as well as in your august presence, I took the oath to perform the duties which, according to the law, are entrusted to the President:

Safeguarding the official religion, the Islamic Republic and the Constitution;

Serving the people and national progress and elevation;

Promotion of religion and morality;

Upholding righteousness and promoting justice;

Desisting from authoritarianism;

Protecting the freedom and dignity of individuals and the rights of the nation;

Safeguarding the territorial integrity and political, economic and cultural independence of the country;

Holding power as a sacred trust from the people and passing it on to the next elected President.

This oath is a religiously binding commitment. As defined in Islam, such oaths or vows must be taken with the purest intentions and with the intent and resolve to fulfill them. And the person taking the oath must, in potential and deed, be capable of fulfilling his religious undertaking.

The responsibilities enumerated in the presidential oath refer to social duties. Hence, with respect to collective responsibilities, the individual assumes undertakings whose fulfillment goes far beyond his individual capabilities. And as such, it is only public resolve and national solidarity that can make the performance of such heavy undertakings possible.

The epic participation of the noble and discerning people of Iran in this round of elections encourages me to claim that the entire nation has joined hands in unison for the fulfillment of the provisions and commitments of this oath, and intends to lay the foundations for a better tomorrow for Islamic Iran. Such a will and resolve on the part of the people and the authorities, to help the government while monitoring and overseeing its performance in action, is indeed a great asset and will certainly serve to facilitate the fulfillment of official responsibilities as well as mutual duties and obligations of government and the people.

On governance and the relations between the ruler and the ruled, Imam Ali (peace be upon him) directs the people to the following:

Do not praise me, so that I can fulfill the rights that are left unrealized and perform the obligations that are left undone.

Do not address me the way despots are addressed, and do not avoid me as the ill-tempered are treated.

Do not approach me with an air of artificiality, and do not think that I find the truth offensive.

I do not want you to revere me.

He who finds listening to complaints difficult will

surely find administration of justice even more so.
Therefore, do not hesitate in telling the truth or in
advising me on matters of justice.

I am neither above fallibility nor am I immune to
error in my conduct, unless God safeguards me
from the self, over which He commands more
control than I.

Such being the case in the eyes of Imam Ali (peace
be upon him), the infallible exemplar of justice of all
times, undoubtedly it is much more difficult for common human beings like us. Therefore, towards the fulfillment of the commitments that lie beyond individual
capability or even that of the government by itself, I seek
guidance and grace from God Almighty and help and
support from the noble people of Iran.

The Leadership, with his unique position in the system and society, and his supervision of the three
branches of government, will undoubtedly guide and
assist us in performing these duties. Likewise, the
esteemed senior religious scholars and jurisprudents will
assist the government in serving the people with their
kind counsel and prayers.

I seek assistance from the Islamic Consultative
Assembly, which embodies the virtues of the nation and
constitutes the body to legislate and supervise the imple-

mentation of laws. Through exercising their legal duty to supervise the performance and conduct of government institutions and authorities and by presenting useful and constructive suggestions, distinguished members of parliament can contribute to the welfare of the nation and more efficient administration of the country, and thus achieve God's blessings and salvation.

I expect the honorable Judiciary to assist the Executive branch in the management of a safe, secure, and just society founded on the rule of law.

I also call on political institutions and organizations, associations, the media, scholars and researchers, academicians and educators, experts and specialists, all men and women of science, letters, culture, and art, and all citizens in all walks of life to help us with their continuous supervision and candid presentation of their demands and views. I call on all to increase the extent of public participation in national policy making at the macro level through continuous evaluation and critique of programs, policies and performances. Certainly, a higher level of involvement and participation by experts in the process of government policy making not only facilitates the fulfillment of mutual duties and obligations of the government and the people, but is also conducive to the realization of the people's most fundamental right, the right to determine their own destiny.

To attain this objective, the government is obligated to provide a safe environment for the exchange of ideas and views within the framework of the criteria set by Islam and the Constitution. The government must promote the culture and capacity for participation, evaluation, critique, and reform. It must itself be the model for tolerance and take the lead in empowerment of the people for participation. For the realization of these objectives, God willing, the main thrust of the overall policies of the Executive branch will be based on:

Institutionalizing the rule of law;
Vigorous pursuit of justice as an exalted religious value and the pivotal factor for social trust, stability, progress, and prosperity;
Promoting and consolidating the principle of accountability which will improve performance while facilitating the intellectual, political, and social advancement of the population;
Empowering the people in order to achieve and ensure an ever-increasing level of their discerning participation.

It is my hope that this great responsibility will be successfully fulfilled through popular participation and coordination among the three branches of government.

The government's belief in the necessity of promoting and consolidating the rule of law in individual and social interactions will in itself expand the possibilities for a higher level of coordination among the Executive, the Legislature, and the Judiciary.

When the government relies on the law in order to serve the people and ensure their participation on a continuous basis, and simultaneously the Legislature is committed to the execution of its paramount role of legal monitoring and supervision of the country's administration, the development of a proper political structure in the society may be attained.

Therefore, establishment of the rule of law is an Islamic, revolutionary, and national obligation, and an absolute imperative, which requires a conducive and enabling environment as well as legal means and instruments coupled with public involvement and assistance.

Out of deep conviction in such a necessity, I presented a program upon entering the presidential campaign which I expected to form the basis of the people's understanding, appraisal, and support, and it is hoped eventually, the covenant between the President and the nation. The outline and the essence of my program was inspired by the provisions of the oath I just took. Our honorable people's vote in this election, a vote for the proposed program, has further underlined the necessity of serious attention to these concepts and elements and more importantly, their implementation.

The Constitution obligates the President with

Safeguarding the official religion, the Islamic
Republic and the Constitution;
Promoting religion and morality;
Upholding righteousness and the promotion of justice.

This is a clear indication of the paramount importance and priority of religion and spirituality in our system. The Islamic revolution is an invitation to the revival of monotheistic thinking and the preponderance of Islamic belief and conduct. It is indeed our unique honor that such a great revolution with far-reaching dimensions and implications was led to victory by a Mujahid jurisprudent, a revolutionary mystic, and a statesman immersed in moral virtues.

Ever since its establishment, the Government of the Islamic Republic of Iran has always felt duty-bound to base its programs and policies on the essence and objectives of Islam, to ensure their compatibility with religious norms and edicts, to prepare the necessary grounds for the promotion of Islamic thinking and spirituality, to eliminate moral decadence and vice from society, and to conduct all executive planning and policy making with the spirit of justice. The pertinent institutions of the Islamic Republic have been active in promoting the observance of religious norms and precepts.

It should be borne in mind, however, that in practice only through internalized perpetuation of divine values can the individual and society attain salvation.

To this end, the criteria and yardsticks for ethics and behavior, and for social relations and conduct, should be the same values and teachings the Holy Prophet of Islam (peace be upon him) has received through revelation and relayed to humankind. Hence, as indicated by the late Imam Khomeini, we should always consider the elements of time and place in the question of Islamic *Ijtihad* [independent interpretation of Islamic jurisprudence] and understand Islam in such a manner that it can respond to and meet emerging issues and needs of all times. We should all avoid considering our own understandings and interpretations as absolute, which can only be attributed to the Book and the Divine Revelation itself.

Under the Islamic system, justice and the welfare of mankind should prevail. To this end, reason and intellect are to be utilized. The best way for the establishment of justice lies in utilizing the best of research and expertise. It is only through the growth of thinking and intellectual forces in society, and the free exchange of ideas, that the government can choose the best views and ways and arrive at the proper criteria for justice in the sophisticated world of today, given the complex mechanisms governing economic, political, and cultural relations in society.

A morally and materially prosperous individual and society who find the Islamic system capable of providing for their reasonable needs, and protecting their rights and dignity, will develop more devotion and commitment, and this constitutes the single best and most principled way for the promotion of religion. A society that enjoys material and spiritual blessings is the one that reflects the truly attractive image of Islam and the revolution; such a society can indeed be a model for emulation in today's world.

For the government to move in this direction, there is no other way but to extend justice and equity to all economic, social, and cultural spheres. Creating opportunities and ensuring equal access to possibilities and privileges, providing a conducive environment for the realization of potentials, flourishing the talents of men and women in all spheres, alleviating poverty, and provision of decent living conditions for all, particularly the needy and the underprivileged, are among the most imperative obligations of the Islamic government. To eliminate poverty, the national economy should be made strong and robust.

Hence, what we need most is balanced, sustained, and comprehensive development that should be realized in all political, economic, cultural, and scientific spheres.

In our view, there is an organic interdependence between development and justice. Development without justice will lead to ever-widening social gaps, while justice without development will lead to the expansion of poverty.

Therefore, our principal need is balanced, sustained, and comprehensive development in all spheres. Human resources are central in the development process. As a consequence, safeguarding the dignity of humans, human resource development, advancement of culture, higher education, and research in society, as well as provision of proper scientific and technical training, are among the major duties of the government.

Protecting the freedom of individuals and the rights of the nation, which constitute a fundamental obligation of the President upon taking the oath, is an imperative emanating from the exalted worth and dignity of the human person enshrined in our Divine religion. Fulfillment of this responsibility can only be attained through wider popular awareness of their own rights, provision of the necessary conditions for the realization of constitutionally guaranteed liberties, strengthening and expanding the institutions of the civil society, promoting ethics, strengthening the culture of dialogue, discourse, appraisal, and critique, and preventing any violation of integrity, dignity, and constitutional rights, and freedoms of individuals.

Institutionalizing the rule of law and founding social interactions on a legal framework will provide a favorable milieu for the realization of social needs and demands. In a society well acquainted with its own rights and ruled by law, rights and legal constraints of all citizens are recognized and given due attention. In such a society, the state and the people, inter-linked with corresponding rights and obligations, find their respective proper meaning and place. Anybody who lives under the Islamic system and complies with the law is entitled to the rights of life, freedom of expression, enjoyment of a decent living, and participation in social, economic, and political affairs. The state has a duty to safeguard these rights and boundaries and to provide the people with the necessary milieu and means of tranquillity and peace of mind in all public and private spheres of life, advancing the rule of law and consolidating security and stability.

Serving the people and national progress and elevation, and safeguarding the territorial integrity and the political, economic, and cultural independence of the country, constitute other important components of presidential responsibility which emanate from Islamic and human values and which place further obligations upon the Islamic state.

Attention to the living conditions of the people is a paramount principle, vital for the existence and survival of the state. We must believe in the people; we must live with their pain and suffering. Stature of the authorities lies not only in their service to the people but also in considering this to be their primary responsibility. Moreover, strengthening and promoting the spirit of national pride and self-esteem, safeguarding our territorial integrity and national independence, fostering popular vigilance and readiness, and promoting and strengthening the Iranian identity on the basis of Islamic and human values, are among the most pivotal duties of the government.

A proud, prosperous, and independent Iran on the world scene is the common aspiration of all devoted and dedicated Iranians. Hence, it is of utmost importance for the government to devote itself to promoting the national interests and prestige of the Islamic Republic, commensurate with her historical, cultural, geographical, and economic standing. Safeguarding and protecting the rights of all Iranian nationals all over the world, defending the rights of the world's Muslims and the downtrodden, particularly the oppressed people of Palestine, and active participation in collective endeavors toward universal progress and advancement, while resisting wisely and decisively the expansionist policies of the domineering powers, foreign threats, or outside aggression in cultural, political, and military fields, are all important duties.

The government must emphasize that in our world, dialogue among civilizations is an absolute imperative. We shall avoid any course of action that may foster tension. We shall have relations with any state which respects our independence. It is our right to make decisions on the basis of national interest. But we shall stand firm against any power who may seek to impose its will on us.

Desisting from authoritarianism and holding power as a sacred trust are also among the obligations of the President which call attention to the question of the distribution of power in society. The legitimacy of the government stems from the people's vote. And a powerful government, elected by the people, is representative, participatory, and accountable. The Islamic government is the servant of the people and not their master, and it is accountable to the nation under all circumstances.

The people must believe that they have the right to determine their own destiny and that the power of the state is bound by limits and constraints set by law. State authority cannot be attained through coercion and dictatorship. Rather, it must be realized through governing according to the law, respecting all rights and obligations, as well as legal constraints on the exercise of power and authority, empowering people to participate and ensuring their involvement in decision-making.

Popular participation requires the emergence of new and divergent expectations. Meeting such expectations, although entailing some difficulty, can be attained through the presence and involvement of the people themselves. In our Islamic and revolutionary society, which enjoys immense and varied material and spiritual resources, and has to its credit, at various levels, great popular epics and accomplishments, meeting such needs and expectations is far from insurmountable.

Meeting society's demands and expectations, making the relations between the Executive apparatus and the people more simple and transparent, and establishing and maintaining the relations between the government and the people on the basis of mutual honesty, trust, and confidence, will undoubtedly help to ensure the responsible and participatory presence of the people in the future of our nation. With the help of the Almighty, I will endeavor to direct the Executive branch toward preserving and expanding the existing trend of the presence and participation of the entire populace, and ensuring accountability to the nation which is essential for political development, and hence, for the legitimacy of the state, and for sustained comprehensive national development.

Our people are the most precious asset and resource of our state, and their continual presence in all spheres of national administration is an inescapable necessity. It is they who have created epics of victory.

Our contemporary history, from the anti-colonial movements [in the nineteenth century] to the Constitutional Revolution — which we revere and whose anniversary we celebrate today — to the great Islamic Revolution and the Sacred Defense, all bear witness to this fact. It is the people's firm belief and resolute will that has rendered many impossibles possible.

At this new historical chapter in the life of our country, I assert my trust in the Islamic and national will, and in the determination of the entire nation. The vigilance, will, devotion, and commitment of all women and men, particularly the youth, give me more hope in the future. I hope that through the grace of God Almighty, national unity, cooperation of all officials, and government institutions, and coordination among the Executive, the Legislature, and the Judiciary, will help me meet my grave responsibilities and fulfill the provisions of the important oath I just took.

I conclude these words with paying tribute to the

memory of our honorable martyrs and a humble homage to the sacrificing war veterans, proud prisoners of war, heroic devotees of the Revolution, and the respectable families of them all.

And our last call is that all praise be to God, the Cherisher, and Sustainer of the worlds.

Biographical Note ᵔᐤ

Seyyed Muhammad Khatami was elected President of the Islamic Republic of Iran on May 23, 1997, with over two-thirds of the popular vote. He was born in 1942 into a middle-class clerical family in the town of Ardakan, located in the province of Yazd in central Iran. His father, Grand Ayatollah Ruhollah Khatami, was widely respected for his piety and progressive views.

At the age of nineteen, Khatami left Ardakan to pursue religious studies in Qom until 1965, when he entered the University of Isfahan to study philosophy. From this time onward, he became active in Islamic politics. In 1969, he began graduate studies in education at the University of Tehran. Two years later, he returned to Qom to pursue further religious studies in Islamic law, jurisprudence, and philosophy. It was in Qom that he became more immersed in political activity. In 1978, on the eve of the Iranian revolution, he was chosen to lead the Hamburg Islamic Institute in Germany, which played a pivotal role in organizing revolutionary activity among the Iranian diaspora. From 1982 to 1992, he served as minister of Culture and Islamic Guidance. During this period he was also briefly head of the War Information Headquarters. In 1992 he was appointed assistant to the President and head of the National Library of Iran, a position he held until his election to the Presidency.

Mr. Khatami is familiar with German, English, and Arabic. He has published two books: *Bim-e Mowj (Fear of the Wave)*, 1993, and *Az Donya-ye Shahr ta Shahr-e Donya (From the City-World to the World-City)*, 1994. He is particularly interested in the works of Farabi, Molla-Sadra, Sheykh Ansari, and Hafez. He is married and has three children.